China's Banking System: Issues for Congress

Michael F. Martin
Specialist in Asian Affairs

February 20, 2012

Congressional Research Service

7-5700

www.crs.gov

R42380

CRS Report for Congress
Prepared for Members and Committees of Congress

Summary

China's banking system has been gradually transformed from a centralized, government-owned and government-controlled provider of loans into an increasingly competitive market in which different types of banks, including several U.S. banks, strive to provide a variety of financial services. Only three banks in China remain fully government-owned; most banks have been transformed into mixed ownership entities in which the central or local government may or may not be a major equity holder in the bank.

The main goal of China's financial reforms has been to make its banks more commercially driven in their operations. However, China's central government continues to wield significant influence over the operations of many Chinese banks, primarily through the activities of the People's Bank of China (PBOC), the China Banking Regulatory Commission (CBRC), and the Ministry of Finance (MOF). In addition, local government officials often attempt to influence the operations of Chinese banks.

Despite the financial reforms, allegations of various forms of unfair or inappropriate competition have been leveled against China's current banking system. Some observers maintain that China's banks remain under government-control, and that the government is using the banks to provide inappropriate subsidies and assistance to selected Chinese companies. Others claim that Chinese banks are being afforded preferential treatment by the Chinese government, given them an unfair competitive advantage over foreign banks trying to enter China's financial markets.

While some question what they characterize as unfair competition in China's banking sector, others are concerned that many of China's banks may be insolvent and that China may experience a financial crisis. According to these commentators, efforts to resolve a serious accumulation of non-performing loans (NPLs) only disguised the problem. In addition, China's NPL situation may have been worsened by its November 2008 stimulus program and the emergence of "local government funding platforms" that generated an estimated $1.7 trillion in local government debt. A financial crisis in the city of Wenzhou revealed the previously underappreciated risk associated with China's "underground" banking activities. Some analysts fear that a sharp decline in China's property values could precipitate a financial crisis that could effect the U.S. economy.

China's banking system raises two key issues that may be of interest to Congress. First, Congress may choose to examine allegations of inappropriate bank subsidies to major Chinese companies, particularly state-owned enterprises (SOEs). Second, under its WTO accession agreement, China was to open its domestic financial markets to foreign banks. Congress may consider reviewing China's compliance with the WTO agreement and press the Obama Administration to raise the issue with the Chinese government.

This report will be updated as circumstances warrant.

Contents

Tables

Appendixes

Contacts

Introduction

Recent developments in China's banking system may have important implications for relations with the United States. Some observers assert that the Chinese government is directing Chinese banks to make investments or provide credit as part of a policy to secure access to strategically important natural resources. Another group of researchers maintain that China's lending practices are providing Chinese companies with an unfair advantage in global markets. Other analysts are concerned that the inefficiencies of the lending practices of Chinese banks may be feeding speculative bubbles in China's real estate and stock markets and/or creating a growing pool of non-performing loans (NPFs) that could precipitate an economic crisis in China that could affect the United States.

China's economic reforms have increased the role its banks are playing in the nation's economy and the government's economic policy. To match the nation's macroeconomic changes, the Chinese government has begun the process of transforming its banking sector from a government-directed system to a more commercially-driven system, characterized in part by market-based allocation mechanisms. At present, China's banks operate in a hybrid world in which they are at time encouraged to make decisions based on commercial considerations, and at other times expected to abide by government directives.

The transitional state of China's banking system has given rise to several concerns about the implications for the China's financial system, China's economy, as well as the global economy. First, some U.S. banks interested in competing in China's domestic market think that Chinese banks are provided an unfair advantage under the current regulatory regime, and that China has not fulfilled its obligations under its World Trade Organization (WTO) accession agreement to open its financial market to foreign competition. Second, it is unclear to what extent China's banks operate based on commercial considerations and to what extent they are vehicles by which the Chinese government advances its political and/or economic agenda. Third, some observers question the efficiency and solvency of China's banking system, given the manner in which it appears to be allocating credit. Fourth, other observers maintain that the Chinese government is utilizing its banks to subsidize key companies and industries to enhance their competitiveness on the global market.

This report begins with a summary of the current status of China's banking sector and the government's banking regulatory system. It then addresses each of the four concerns listed above, with a focus on the implications for U.S. relations with China. The report concludes with a discussion of the main implications for Congress.

China's Banking Sector

Prior to the beginning of China's economic reforms in 1978, the Chinese banking system was largely government-owned and isolated from the global economy. China's banks were generally subservient to the requirements of China's central planned economy. A gradual process of change has created a banking system in China with multiple categories of institutions and agencies, operating in separated markets with generally clearly delineated functions. One of the main objectives of China's banking reforms has been to create incentives for its financial institutions to behave more like competitive, commercial entities. Competition between these financial institutions and agencies is usually limited to those performing similar functions, but cross function rivalries do exist. However, China's banks have not been granted complete autonomy, and are frequently required to comply with government directives with serious implications for their profitability and in some cases, their solvency.

Several categories of banks operate in China, with different ownership structures and serving different functions. The first category includes wholly state-owned banks. The second category consists of "equitized" commercial banks – banks that were previously wholly state-owned, but were transformed into joint-stock companies, in which the Chinese central government is usually the largest stockholder.[1] The third category encompasses a variety of local banks, with provincial or municipal governments as major stockholders. A fourth category is composed of Chinese joint-stock commercial banks that were created after the start of China's banking reforms and with comparatively low levels of government ownership. Below is a discussion of the main characteristics of each category, including the names of the major banks in each category. A more complete list of Chinese banks by type is provided at the end of this report (see **Appendix**). In addition to the legal banks, China also has an unknown number of illegal banking operations, or "underground banks," that accept deposits and offer loans to individuals and businesses (see "Underground Banks").

Wholly State-Owned Policy Banks

China's banking sector was previously dominated by four wholly state-owned policy banks—the Agricultural Bank of China (ABC), the Bank of China (BOC), China Construction Bank (CCB), and the Industrial and Commercial Bank of China (ICBC). In addition, there were several other smaller wholly state-owned policy banks, such as Bank of Communications, China Development Bank (also known as the State Development Bank of China), the Export Import Bank of China (China Exim Bank), and Huaxia Bank. Starting in 2005, China began transforming the wholly state-owned banks into joint-stock corporations, a process it calls "equitization" (see section on "Equitized Banks"), that were to operate as commercial banks. As a result, only three wholly-state owned banks remain in China—the Agricultural Development Bank of China, China Development Bank and China Exim Bank. China Development Bank is reportedly to be equitized sometime in the near future, but plans for its initial public offering (IPO) have been on hold for over two years. There are no reported plans to equitize the Agricultural Development Bank of China or China Exim Bank.

Each of the three remaining state-owned banks have a distinct mission. The main mission of Agricultural Development Bank of China (中国农业发展银行, or ADBC) is to support the development of agriculture and rural areas in China. China Development Bank (国家开发银行, or CDB) traditionally was responsible for raising funds for large infrastructure projects, but over the last few years, the CDB has begun to diversify its portfolio of investments as part of its transition into a commercial bank. The main purpose of China Exim Bank (中国进出口银行) is to provide financial services to promote Chinese exports (particularly of high-tech and new-tech products) and facilitate the import of technologically advanced machinery and equipment. All three banks have a board of directors and senior officers, appointed by China's cabinet, the State Council. All three state-owned commercial banks report directly to the State Council, and frequently rely on the State Council's directives in establishing their operational priorities.

---

[1] Other authors refer to these banks as being "corporatized." This report will utilize the term most frequently used in the Chinese press, "equitized."

Equitized Banks

Five of the previously state-owned policy banks have been transformed into joint-stock companies, with different categories of shareholders, and are supposedly operating as commercial banks. For four of the five equitized banks the majority of the shares are non-tradable shares held by the People's Bank of China (PBOC), the Ministry of Finance (MOF), or other government entities, raising questions about their degree of separation from government control (see**Table 1**). In addition, some of the non-tradable shares are held by foreign banks.

Table 1. Size and Ownership of China's Equitized Commercial Banks

Latest available figures

Bank	Market Capital	State Holdings of Outstanding Shares	Major U.S. Holdings of Outstanding Shares
Agricultural Bank of China (ABC)	$1.019 trillion	83.13%	None
Bank of China (BOC)	$1.084 trillion	67.53%	None
Bank of Communications	$398 billion	26.52%	None
China Construction Bank (CCB)	$1.717 trillion	57.0%	Bank of America – 10.9%
Industrial and Commercial Bank of China (ICBC)	$1.810 trillion	70.7%	American Express – 0.2%
			Goldman Sachs – 4.9%

Sources: home pages of banks; DBS Vickers Securities, "China Banking Sector," May 19, 2009.

Tradable shares of the equitized banks—typically representing only a fraction of the total equity of the bank—are sold on China's two stock markets (Shanghai and Shenzhen) to Chinese investment funds, qualified foreign institutional investors (QFIIs),[2] and private Chinese investors, and on the Hong Kong Stock Exchange to overseas investors.[3]

Previously, when they were wholly state-owned, the equitized commercial banks had assigned financial responsibilities. After their conversion to joint-stock companies, the banks have diversified their financial services to include corporate and personal financial services. The equitized commercial banks are also investing overseas.

The intent of equitizating the state-owned commercial banks was to create the space and the incentives for the officers of each bank to operate it as a for-profit commercial bank with less interference from China's central government. Each of the equitized banks has a board of directors and senior officers, who are generally appointed in some fashion by the central government. Results to date have been mixed, but the equitized commercial banks are among the

---

[2] The concept of qualified foreign institutional investors, or QFIIs, was created by the Chinese government in 2002 to allow selected foreign investors a means by which they could purchase RMB-denominated shares of Chinese companies (the so-called "A shares") in the Shanghai or Shenzhen stock markets. As of July 2011, the China Securities Regulatory Commission (CSRC) had licensed 113 QFIIs with a combined investment limit of $20 billion.

[3] Shares sold in Shanghai and Shenzhen are frequently referred to as A Shares and B Shares, respectively; shares sold in Hong Kong are called H Shares. A and B shares are denominated in renminbi; H shares in Hong Kong dollars. Because the shares sell in separate markets, their prices may diverge from each other.

most dynamic and innovative financial institutions in China. Because of their size, the five equitized commercial banks continue to dominate China's banking sector.

Local Banks

The category of local banks includes a variety of financial institutions. The largest category is commonly known as "city commercial banks." Over the years, some provincial and municipal governments established their own banks (such as Guangdong Development Bank and Shanghai Pudong Development Bank). These banks were wholly-owned by the local government and were used by the local government to handle locally developed projects and programs. Since the turn of the century, they have been gradually transformed into joint-stock companies where the local government is often the largest shareholder. As of 2009, an average of 18.5% of the shares of city commercial banks were owned by local governments. The majority of the shares were owned by other Chinese banks or corporations, foreign banks, and a restricted amount by bank employees and private investors.[4] According to the CBRC's most recent annual report, there were 147 "city commercial banks" in China as of the end of 2010.[5] **Appendix** provides a partial list of China's city commercial banks taken from the CBRC's webpage.[6]

Because of their smaller size, these city commercial banks struggle to compete with the larger state-owned policy banks and the equitized banks. However, due to their past ties to the local government, the city commercial banks often benefit by being chosen by the local government to handle the province's or city's finances or manage the government's pensions funds and other government-related accounts. In addition, the city commercial banks often are better able to assess the credit-worthiness of local companies. Competition with the larger equitized banks and private commercial banks has made some of city commercial banks among the most innovative financial institutions in China.

Local banks also include village and township banks, rural commercial banks, rural cooperative banks, and rural credit cooperatives. Starting in 2004, the Chinese government began the process of transforming the rural credit cooperatives into joint-stock companies. The CBRC launched a three-year plan in 2009 to open nearly 1,300 new rural financial institutions, including over 1,000 rural banks, by the end of 2011. In September 2010, the CBRC announced that domestic banks could buy 100% of existing rural credit cooperatives, and private and foreign investors could purchase up to 20%.[7] As of the end of 2010, there were 349 village and township banks, 85 rural commercial banks, 223 rural cooperative banks, and 2,646 rural credit cooperatives in China.[8] By and large, the various rural financial institutions only provide services to China's rural population.

---

[4] In August 2010, the China Banking Regulatory Commission and the China Securities Regulatory Commission limited the share holdings of employees to 10% for any local bank wishing to issue shares or wanting to be listed on either the Shanghai or Shenzhen stock exchange.

[5] China Banking Regulatory Commission, *Annual Report 2010*, April 2011, p. 26.

[6] http://www.cbrc.gov.cn/english/info/yjhjj/index_links.jsp?s=dbi

[7] "China Puts Rural Credit Cooperatives on Sale," *Reuters*, September 1, 2010.

[8] China Banking Regulatory Commission, *Annual Report 2010*, April 2011, p. 26.

"Private" Commercial Banks

There are two types of "private" commercial banks in China—12 Chinese-owned joint-stock commercial banks and a growing number of foreign-owned banks. The largest and best-known Chinese joint-stock commercial bank is China Minsheng Bank (中国民生银行). China Minsheng Bank was established in Beijing in 1996, and was the first joint-stock commercial bank in which the majority of the shares were owned by non-governmental entities. As of June 2008, China Minsheng Bank had 29 branches distributed across China.

According to CBRC, 37 wholly foreign-owned banks, plus two foreign joint-venture banks and one wholly foreign-owned finance companies, had incorporated in China as of the end of 2010 with a combined total of 270 branches or subsidiaries (see **Table 2**). In addition, 90 foreign banks had chosen to open branches of their home bank in China. As a result, 360 separate foreign banking establishments were operating in China by the end of 2010 in 45 cities and 27 provinces across the country. The combined assets of these institutions was valued at $1.74 trillion yuan (approximately $274 billion), or 1.83% of total banking assets in China.[9]

According to a June 2010 PriceWaterhouseCoopers study of foreign banks in China, the emerging product range available in China, including RMB bonds, is making local incorporation more attractive.[10] However, local incorporation is expensive; a foreign bank that wishes to incorporate in China must have a minimum registered capital in China of 1 billion yuan ($157 million) plus an additional 100 million yuan ($14.6 million) for each branch. In addition, new regulations issued by the CBRC require locally incorporated banks to maintain a 75% loan-to-deposit ratio by the end of 2011.

Table 2. Foreign Banking Establishments in China

As of end of 2010

	Foreign Banks	Wholly Foreign-Owned Banks Incorporated in China	Joint Venture Banks Incorporated in China	Wholly Foreign-Owned Finance Companies Incorporated in China
Number of Entities	N/A	37	2	I
Branches or Subsidiaries	90	260	9	I

Source: China Banking Regulatory Commission, *2010 Annual Report*, April 2011.

Underground Banks

A variety of entities operate illegally in China as underground banks (地下钱庄), also know as "shadow banking."[11] Some of China's credit guarantee agencies have moved beyond their

---

[9] Unless otherwise noted, this report will use the prevailing official exchange rate on November 28, 2011, which was 6.3585 yuan per U.S. dollar.

[10] PriceWaterhouseCoopers, *Foreign Banks in China*, May 2010.

[11] For an overview of the types of institutions involved in underground banking, see Nicholas Borst, "China Shadow Banking Primer," *China Economic Watch*, Peterson Institute for International Economics, November 1, 2011.

intended purpose to effectively become banks, taking deposits and providing loans (see "Credit Guarantee Agencies" sidebar). Similarly, some investment brokers and private fund managers in China have used their available capital to provide illegal commercial and personal loans. In addition, some pawn shops are providing illegal banking services to people and businesses unable or unwilling to use the legal banking system.[12]

China's underground banks have emerged for several reasons. Some people choose to deposit their funds with the underground banks because they offer higher deposit rates than legal banks. Other people may use the underground banks to conceal their wealth from authorities. Some businesses – particularly small and medium-sized companies – may apply for loans from underground banks because they cannot obtain a loan from legal banks or the approval process takes too long.[13]

> ### Credit Guarantee Agencies
>
> In the 1990s, the Chinese government authorized the creation of credit guarantee agencies. These agencies were created to improve access to credit for small and medium-sized business that had trouble obtaining loans from banks. The idea was that these businesses would be more able to receive approval for their loan applications if the credit guarantee agencies ensured that the bank would be repaid for the loan. China's credit guarantee agencies have grown rapidly, with an estimated 5,000 in operation at the end of 2010. The credit guarantee agencies have also proven to be attractive to foreign investors seeking entry into China's financial markets.

While the underground banks provide access to credit to individual and businesses with little or no chance of being approved for a loan by a legal bank, the credit comes at a cost. Interest rates on loans provided by China's underground banks are often 10% per month or higher. As a result, borrowers tend to use the underground banks mainly for short-term loans in order to avoid substantial interest charges. Another cost of doing business with underground banks is dealing with their sometimes unorthodox methods to obtain overdue loan payments, such as kidnapping family members.[14]

China's Ministry of Finance and the State Administration of Foreign Exchange (SAFE) have been cracking down on underground banks primarily because they are seen as a major conduit for the illegal flow of overseas capital into China. Since 2002, the Chinese authorities have shut down over 500 underground banks, with over 100 cases involving more than 200 billion yuan ($31 billion) in illegal funds.[15]

While officially outside of China's banking system, the potential importance of underground banks was made apparent in early October, when the network of private financing in the city of Wenzhou in Zhejiang Province threatened to collapse and possibly precipitate a regional credit crisis. According to one report, a central bank survey of Wenzhou found that about 60% of local businesses and most households had loans with the city's underground banks.[16] Unable to service their debts, a number of private business owners fled the city, leaving behind unpaid workers and outstanding bills. According to some accounts, some of the funding for Wenzhou's underground

---

[12] "Small, Mid-sized Companies Turn to Pawnshops for Loans," *China Daily*, February 16, 2011.

[13] For an overview of China's underground banking, see Nicholas Borst, *China Shadow Banking Primer*, Peterson Institute for International Economics, Washington, DC, November 1, 2011.

[14] Andrew Moody and Hu Haiyan, "Cash Crunch Delivers a Knock-out Blow," *China Daily- USA Weekly*, January 6-12, 2012.

[15] "China Shuts Down 500 Underground Banks in 8 Years: Ministry," *Xinhua*, November 22, 2010.

[16] Zhang Bing, Zheng Fei, and Zhao Jingting, "Cash Crash for Wnezhou's Private Loan Network," *Caixin*, November 10, 2011.

banks came from commercial loans obtained by local businesses from legitimate commercial banks. The mounting defaults on the underground loans raised the risk that these businesses would be unable to service their loans to the commercial banks.

The Wenzhou underground banking crisis was considered sufficiently important that Premier Wen Jiabao, PBOC Governor Zhou Xiaochuan, and Finance Minister Xie Xuren visited the city to assess the situation. Preliminary results indicated that the prevalence of underground financing was unusually high in Wenzhou, and that the local credit crisis posed no serious threat to China's banking system. However, following the officials' visit, the CBRC announced that it was looking into ways to curb the use of underground banks.[17]

Market Share

Although the Chinese banking system contains a variety of types of banks, its market is dominated by the five equitized banks (see **Table 3**). Just under half of the total assets in China's banking sector are owned by these five banks—Agricultural Bank of China (ABC), Bank of China (BOC), Bank of Communications, China Construction Bank (CCB), and Industrial and Commercial Bank of China (ICBC)—providing each bank with a significant share of the overall market. The 12 joint-stock commercial banks are the second largest group, with 15.6% of the market, which gives each of the 12 banks a small, but notable portion of the market. The 147 city commercial banks have 8.2% of banking assets. Except in some of China's more economically advanced cities, these banks play a minor role in the national financial markets. The over 3,300 rural financial institutions have the third largest share of the market (11.2%), but the holdings of each individual institution are extremely small.

Table 3. Market Share of Types of Banks in China

By total assets at the end of 2010

Type of Bank	Asset Value	Market Share
Policy Banks	7.652 trillion yuan	8.0%
Equitized Banks	46.894 trillion yuan	49.2%
City Commercial Banks	7.853 trillion yuan	8.2%
Rural Commercial Banks, Rural Cooperative Banks, and Rural Credit Cooperatives	10.658 trillion yuan	11.2%
Joint-stock Commercial Banks	14.904 trillion yuan	15.6%
Foreign Banks	1.742 trillion yuan	1.8%
Other	5.602 trillion yuan	5.9%

Source: Based on data in CBRC's *Annual Report 2010.*

---

[17] "China to Control Shadow Banking and Private Lending," *BBC*, October 19, 2011.

China's Banking Regulatory System

Under China's current banking regulatory system, four key entities report to China's ruling State Council (中华人民共和国国务院), each with its own distinct area of responsibility. China's central bank is the People's Bank of China (PBOC), which is responsible for formulating and implementing China's monetary policy. The PBOC and the China Banking Regulatory Commission (CBRC) effectively oversee the operations of all banking institutions in China. The Ministry of Finance (MoF) is responsible for China's fiscal policies and the central government's budget. The State Administration of Foreign Exchange (SAFE) is responsible for the supervision and monitoring of foreign exchange transactions in China, as well as the management of the government's foreign exchange reserves. Below is a short description of each of these four entities.

People's Bank of China

Following the creation of the People's Republic of China in 1949, the new Chinese government nationalized all the banks under the People's Bank of China (中国人民银行), or the PBOC. Between 1949 and 1978, the PBOC was administratively under the authority of the Ministry of Finance. In 1979, the PBOC became a separate entity, reporting directly to the State Council. In addition, the banking functions of the PBOC were transferred over to three state-owned policy banks—the Agricultural Bank of China (中国农业银行, or ABC), the Bank of China (中国银行, or BOC), and the People's Construction Bank of China (中国人民建设银行, or PCBC), which was later renamed China Construction Bank (中国建设银行, or CCB). A fourth state-owned policy bank, the Industrial and Commercial Bank of China (中国工商银行, or ICBC), was formed in 1984.

Initially, these four state-owned policy banks were under the direct authority of the PBOC. Starting in 2005, China began a process of transforming them into joint-stock commercial banks—a process it calls "equitization" (see section on "Equitized Banks"). All of the four policy banks—ABC, BOC, CCB, and ICBC—have been equitized.

Following the transfer of its banking functions to the state-owned commercial banks, the PBOC's main purpose was as China's central bank. According to the PBOC's web page (www.pbc.gov.cn), its "major responsibilities" are:

- Formulating and implementing monetary policy;

- Issuing renminbi (RMB, or 人民币,[18] China's currency, and regulating its circulation;

- Regulating the inter-bank lending and bond markets;

- Administering foreign exchange and regulating the inter-bank foreign exchange market;

- Regulating the gold market;

---

[18] The official name of China's currency is *renminbi*, or "people's currency." It is denominated in units called *yuan* (元). One *yuan* is divided into 10 *jiao* (角), popularly known as *mao* (毛), or 100 *fen* (分). Some publications refer to China's currency as the *yuan*, conflating the name of the currency with its unit of denomination.

- Holding and managing official foreign exchange and gold reserves;

- Managing the state treasury (including the issuance of treasury bonds and other government securities);

- Operating the payment and settlement system;

- Maintaining financial statistics and conducting financial analysis and forecasts;

- Guiding and organizing anti-money laundering operations; and

- Issuing and enforcing relevant orders and regulations.

As the main administrator of monetary policy, the PBOC manages the traditional instruments of monetary policy: setting reserve requirements for banks and other financial institutions, setting the discount rate (interest rate) for intra-bank lending; and controlling the supply of money (via the issuance of currency and open market operations). In addition, the PBOC utilizes two regulatory tools not available to the U.S. Federal Reserve—the setting of benchmark interest rates for RMB-denominated deposits and loans, and the allocation of credit limits to Chinese banks.[19]

In contrast to the U.S. Federal Reserve, the PBOC tends to utilize changes in the banks' reserve requirements as its primary method of signaling its desire to tighten or loosen bank lending, and thereby, the money supply. For example, in 2010 and much of 2011, the PBOC was concerned about the rising rate of inflation. In response, the PBOC increased the reserve requirement ratio six times in 2010 and another six times in the first half of 2011.[20] Each time, the reserve requirement was increased by 0.5%, resulting in a 6.0% total increase in 18 months. As of June 20, 2011, China's reserve requirement stood at 21.5%.[21] On August 25, 2011, the PBOC announced an expansion of its deposit reserve requirements to cover previously exempt types of accounts in an effort to block avenues by which banks had circumvented the tightening of the money supply.[22] Despite these actions by the PBOC, China's consumer price index (CPI) remained relatively high. In June 2011, the official CPI was up 6.4% year-on-year, and rose to 6.5% in July.

The PBOC also uses changes in benchmark interest rates for deposits and loans in its monetary policy, but with less frequency than changes in the reserve requirement. Under Chinese law and regulation, banks are allowed to offer interest rates within a band above and below the benchmark rates.[23] As a result, the PBOC benchmark rates and their corresponding permissible bands have a limited effect on banks' interest rates.

---

[19] The PBOC is also responsible for China's exchange rate policy, but that function will not be addressed in this report.

[20] From CRS interviews with officials at Chinese banks, it is unclear if the banks view increases of the reserve requirement as an effort to reduce inflation by encouraging banks to reduce lending.

[21] By comparison, the Federal Reserves' current reserve requirement for "net transaction accounts" (demand deposits, automatic transfer service (ATS) accounts, NOW accounts, and other highly liquid accounts) is 10% on holdings above $58.8 million. On December 5, 2011, PBOC reduced the reserve requirement by 50 basis points, the first cut since December 25, 2008.

[22] The types of accounts included margin deposits, letters of guarantee, bills of exchange, and letters of credit. For more information, see Wang Shenlu, "Central Bank Swerves to Block Deposit Detours," *Caixin*, September 7, 2011.

[23] The size of the band varies for different types of interest rates. For example, bank lending rates can be no less than 90% of the benchmark rate set by the PBOC, with no upward limit. Following the devastating Wenchuan earthquake in May 2008, the PBOC lowered the floor mortgage rate to 70% of the benchmark rate.

The PBOC raised benchmark interest rates twice in 2010, compared to six increases in the reserve requirement. On July 7, 2011, the PBOC raised the benchmark interest rate on one-year time deposits to 3.5% and the one-year lending rate to 6.56% in an effort to curb inflation (see **Table 4**), the third such increase in 2011.[24] Each time the PBOC raised the one-year deposit and loan rates by 0.25%, preserving the 3.06% spread between the two rates.

Table 4. Benchmark Interest Rates for Deposits and Loans

by duration, as of July 7, 2011

Deposits	6 month	1 year	2 years	3 years	5 years
	3.30%	3.50%	4.40%	5.00%	5.50%
Loans	6 month	1 year	1-3 years	3-5 years	Over 5 years
	6.10%	6.56%	6.65%	6.90%	7.05%

Source: People's Bank of China, "PBC Decides to Raise RMB Benchmark Deposit and Loan Rates," July 6, 2011.

Another way the PBOC has historically restricted the commercial activities of banks is by allocating credit quotas to banks. In the past, the Chinese government would announce a target for the growth of credit for the year, and the PBOC would then allocate the available credit among China's banks. The PBOC did not publicly announced credit quotas for 2011, but reportedly provided banks with "target" growth rates of 13 or 14% for credit for the year.[25] According to the PBOC, total outstanding loans in China rose by 15.7% in 2011, slightly above the target rate.[26]

Under the leadership of Governor Zhou Xiaochuan,[27] the PBOC has generally supported the liberalization of China's banking sector. Governor Zhou released a statement on December 17, 2010 on "market-based interest rate reform" in which he advocated a policy to gradually adopting competitively set interest rates. In the article, he notes that starting from 1992, banks in China have been given more autonomy in setting interest rates. By 2010, wrote Governor Zhou, "all financial institutions but policy ones operate on a fully commercial basis, and an important part of their autonomy is to independently price their products and services."[28]

China Banking Regulatory Commission

Following the Asian Financial Crisis of 1997,[29] China created the China Banking Regulatory Commission (中国银行业监督管理委员会 or CBRC). In contrast to the PBOC, which manages monetary policy, the CBRC is responsible for the regulatory oversight of China's banks, ensuring

---

[24] Historically, the PBOC has maintained a roughly 3% range between comparable deposit and loan benchmark rates, thereby insuring banks approximately a 3% gross profit margin.

[25] Wang Bo, "14% Credit Growth Predicted for 2011," *China Daily*, December 23, 2010.

[26] People's Bank of China, "Financial Statistics, 2011," press release, January 12, 2012.

[27] Zhou Xiaochuan (周小川) was appointed Governor of PBOC in December 2002. He is considered a close associate of ex-Premier Zhu Rongji (朱镕基) and ex-General Secretary of the Chinese Communist Party (CCP) Jiang Zemin (江泽民).

[28] Zhou Xiaochuan, "A Few Thoughts on Market-based Interest Rate Reform," December 17, 2010.

[29] For an analysis of the Asian Financial Crisis of 1997, see CRS Report 98-434, *The Asian (Global?) Financial Crisis, the IMF, and Japan: Economic Issues*, by Dick K. Nanto.

that they are abiding by the relevant laws and regulations, and that the interests of depositors and consumers are protected. Its main functions are to: authorize the establishment and business scope of banks in China; formulate and enforce banking regulations; audit and supervise all banks operating in China; and compile and publish information on China's banking sector.

Shang Fuling (尚福林) was appointed as CBRC Chairman on October 29, 2011, by the CCP's Central Committee, replacing Liu Mingkang (刘明康) who had reached the mandatory retirement age of 65. Shang was transferred from the China Securities Regulatory Commission (CSRC), where he had been Chairman since 2002. Shang is credited with successfully guiding China's stock markets through a comparatively tumultuous period by implementing a series of reforms. He is expected to use his experiences with CSRC and past postings in the banking sector to manage China's future banking reforms.

True to its origins, the CBRC has generally been more cautious about the liberalization of China's banking sector. The CBRC sees excessive deregulation and poor oversight by the U.S. government and the Federal Reserve as the principal causes of the 2007-2008 global financial crisis. It is generally dismissive of claims that China was partially responsible for the crisis, and instead, sees China's pre- and post-crisis policies as being a critical element of Asia's quick recovery from the global economic downturn. The CBRC's top priorities for 2012, according to a statement by Chairman Shang, are: 1. defend the bottom line; 2. improve the risk control system; 3. strengthen external supervision and internal controls; 4. deepen financial reform by speeding up product and service innovation (especially for rural areas and small and micro enterprises); 5. promote economic restructuring; and 6. closing down illegal financial activities.[30]

Ministry of Finance

Once the sole authority for China's financial sector, the Ministry of Finance (财政部 MoF) has gradually lost responsibility and authority during the course of China's economic reforms. The MoF's current main functions are to: formulate and implement China's fiscal policies; prepare and administer the central government's annual budget; propose and collect taxes for the central government; prepare plans for the issuance of treasury bonds and other central government debt; formulate and implement accounting regulations for businesses operating in China; collect data; and conduct research on China's economy and its fiscal situation.

In addition to previously supervising the activities of the PBOC, the MoF used to manage several other important financial institutions and entities in China. Although its direct management of other financial institutions has been taken away, the MoF continues to hold some authority over some banks and other financial institutions by means of either its equity holdings and/or having a representative on their governing boards. For example, the MoF holds 50% of the equity in the Agricultural Bank of China.[31] In addition, the views of the MoF are influential with the State Council, which must approve all major banking policies.[32]

---

[30] China Banking Regulatory Commission, "Defend the Bottom Line; Better Serve the Real Economic Development," press release, December 14, 2011.

[31] The other 50% is held by Central Huijin Investments, a wholly-owned subsidiary of China Investment Corporation.

[32] Article 5 of Law of the People's Republic of China on the People's Bank of China, adopted in 1995, requires that the PBOC obtain the approval of the State Council for all its major decisions.

State Administration of Foreign Exchange

Established in 1978, the State Administration of Foreign Exchange (国家外汇管理局 or SAFE), reports to both the State Council and the PBOC. Its main function is to manage China's foreign exchange, including maintaining balance of payments statistics, regulating and monitoring foreign exchange transactions, and managing China's foreign exchange (forex) reserves. As the regulator of foreign exchange transactions, SAFE must approve the outlay of any forex for overseas investments by Chinese banks and companies. As the manager of China's forex reserves, SAFE also acts at times like a bank, providing credit to companies seeking to make overseas investments.

SAFE keeps the details of its investment holdings secret. It generally invests China's foreign exchange reserves in traditional items, such as U.S. Treasury bonds, which are perceived as being relatively safe and fairly liquid. According to one source, 70% of SAFE's assets are in U.S.-dollar denominated bonds.[33] However, there are signs that SAFE is diversifying its investment portfolio. In 2008, SAFE made small investments (usually less than 1% of total outstanding shares) in companies in Australia, France, and the United Kingdom. Among the companies in which SAFE currently holds an equity position are: Barclays, British Gas, Cadbury, Drax Group, Royal Bank of Scotland, Tesco, and Wire & Plastic Products Group.[34]

SAFE is also responsible for the regulation of "qualified foreign institutional investors," or QFIIs. QFIIs are non-Chinese entities that are allowed to purchase stock, bonds and other financial assets in China.[35] Under current regulations, the QFIIs must have an authorized Chinese custodian bank as a partner. Since 2002, China has authorized 103 QFIIs to operate in China; as of April 2011, SAFE had approved $20.69 billion in investment quotas for QFIIs .[36] On May 6, 2011, China Securities Regulatory Commission (中国证券监督管理委员会 or CSRC) published draft regulations allowing QFIIs to trade in stock index futures for hedging purposes.[37]

China's Regulations for Foreign Banks[38]

Under the terms of its 2001 World Trade Organization (WTO) accession agreement, China agreed to gradually open its financial markets over a five year period to foreign competitors. The services schedule of China's WTO accession agreement[39] delineates the details of the scope of foreign bank access to China's financial markets. Foreign banks generally are to be afforded

---

[33] Leona Chen, "Will China Buy into BHP Billiton?" *China Stakes*, April 13, 2008.

[34] Tim Johnston, "Beijing Buys into Australian Banks," *International Herald Tribune*, January 4, 2008.

[35] China has created a domestic counterpart to the QFIIs – the "qualified domestic institutional investors," or QDIIs. The QDIIs are funds by which Chinese individuals can invest overseas.

[36] "The SAFE Approves Investment Quotas for Qualified Institutional Investors in a Prudent and Orderly Manner," press release, State Administration of Foreign Exchange, April 29, 2011.

[37] "China to Allow QFIIs to Trade Stock Index Futures," *Reuters*, May 7, 2011.

[38] Contents of this section are based in part on information provided by the International Trade Administration of the Department of Commerce on its webpages – http://www.mac.doc.gov/China/Docs/industryfactsheets/banking.html and http://www.mac.doc.gov/China/ServicesSchedule.pdf.

[39] Report of the Working Party on the Accession of China, "Addendum, Schedule CLII – The People's Republic of China, Part II – Schedule of Specific Commitments on Services, List of Article II MFN Exemptions," WT/MIN(01)/3/Add.2, November 10, 2001.

---

national treatment for listed banking services, with the ability to provide the same types of services and facing the same legal restrictions as domestic banks. There are, however, some exceptions. For example, foreign banks are not allowed to provide automobile financing. Foreign banks can accept deposits, make loans (including mortgages, consumer credit, factoring, and commercial financing), issue credit and debit cards, provide letters of credit or guaranty, and other financial services.

Since 2001, the Chinese government has passed laws and regulations to implement its WTO obligations. On November 11, 2006, China's State Council promulgated Decree No. 478, "Regulations of the People's Republic of China on Administration of Foreign-funded Banks," establishing the general policy of foreign bank operations in China. The regulations differentiated between "foreign-funded banks" (which includes "wholly foreign-funded banks" and "Chinese-foreign joint venture banks") and their branches, and a branch of a foreign bank. While the types of financial services the two types of foreign banks were authorized to provide were almost identical,[40] they were subject to different minimum capital requirements. Foreign-funded banks had to have a minimum of 1 billion yuan ($157 million) in registered capital and have received a minimum of 100 million yuan ($15.7 million) in non-callable operating capital. Branches of foreign banks operating in China had to have received a minimum of 200 million yuan ($31.5 million) in operating capital. In addition, the owners of foreign-funded banks must possess no less than $10 billion in assets at the end of the year prior to the submission of an application to form a foreign-funded bank, and the foreign banks seeking to establish a branch in China must possess no less than $20 billion in assets at the end of the year prior to the submission of an application to open the branch.

The approval process for foreign-funded banks and branches of foreign banks is a two-step process. The first step is the submission of application documents to China's banking regulatory agencies, which are to make a decision within six months of submission.[41] The second step involves the submission of additional information within six months of receiving the decision of the regulatory agencies. China's banking regulatory agencies have up to two months to approve or reject the second submission. If the application is approved, the applicant must register with the appropriate administrative department and obtain a business license.

If foreign-funded banks or branches of foreign banks intend to apply to provide services denominated in renminbi, the regulations require that the bank have been in operation in China for no less than three years, and have been profitable for two consecutive years prior to the application. Both types of foreign banks must also comply with the asset-liability ratio requirements prescribed in the Law of the People's Republic of China on Commercial Banks.[42] Among these ratios is a requirement that "the ratio of the outstanding of loans to the outstanding of deposits may not exceed 75 percent."

While the 2006 regulations provide greater market access to foreign banks, the Chinese government has also eliminated some of the special privileges previously offered to foreign banks. Special business arrangements – including tax holidays or reductions – were phased out,

---

[40] There were restrictions on the minimum amount (initially, 1 million yuan) a branch of a foreign bank can accept in a time deposit from a Chinese citizen.

[41] The regulations allow for an extension of up to three months "in special circumstances." If there is an extension, the applicant is to be notified in writing.

[42] Text of the law available online at http://www.china.org.cn/english/DAT/214824.htm.

making foreign banks compete and operate under the same conditions as Chinese banks. For example, special tax deductions available to foreign banks for doubtful debts were eliminated on December 31, 2010.

U.S. Banks in China: Limited Market Access

The U.S. government, U.S. banks, and other interested parties are concerned that the Chinese authorities are limiting market access for U.S. banks and protecting Chinese banks from competition from U.S. banks. Although China has made apparent efforts to comply with its WTO obligations, several U.S. banks maintain that China's laws and regulations, and the manner in which they have been enforced, have created barriers to entry for U.S. banks. A recent assessment of China's WTO compliance by the Office of the U.S. Trade Representative (USTR) was generally supportive of the views of U.S. banks.[43]

Table 5. U.S. Banks Operating in China

As of December 2011

Bank	Type of Operations
Bank of America	Branch (3)
Bank of New York Mellon	Branch (2)
Bank of the Orient	Branch (1)
Citibank	Subsidiary, plus branches (49)
East West Bancorp	Branch (2)
JPMorgan Chase	Subsidiary, plus branches (7)
Northern Trust	Branch (1)
Wells Fargo	Branch (1)

Source: U.S. Treasury

Notes: Number in parentheses indicates number of branches.

As of December 2011, eight U.S. banks were operating in China (see **Table 5**). Two banks – Citibank and JPMorgan Chase – chose to establish a subsidiary bank in China. The Chinese government considers these subsidiaries to be wholly foreign-funded banks. The other six U.S. banks established what the Chinese consider branches of a foreign bank. Seven additional banks have opened representative offices in China, but are not offering financial services.[44]

In its 2011 report to Congress on China's WTO compliance, USTR mentioned four shortcomings in China's fulfillment of its WTO obligations related to banking.[45] First, USTR sees the capital requirements for foreign banks as a de-facto barrier to entry. Second, foreign equity ownership

---

[43] Office of the U.S. Trade Representative, *2011 USTR Report to Congress on China's WTO Compliance*, Washington, DC, December 12, 2011.

[44] The six banks are: American Express, Cathay Bank Corporation, Comerica Bank Corporation, Far East National Bank, MetroBank, PNC Bank and State Street Bank and Trust.

[45] Office of the U.S. Trade Representative, *2011 USTR Report to Congress on China's WTO Compliance*, Washington, DC, December 12, 2011.

has been effectively limited to 25% although existing regulations allow for up to 49% for joint venture banks. Third, the requirements for a foreign bank to offer financial services in renminbi are considered overly restrictive. Fourth, the process of obtaining approval to open a new bank or branch is too slow and cumbersome. Previously, USTR filed a WTO case against China in September 2010 for its exclusion of U.S. suppliers from China's electronic payment services market (see "U.S. WTO Case Against China on Electronic Payment Services" sidebar). The USTR report indicated that obtaining "full access to the domestic currency business" for U.S. banks remains a priority.

U.S. banks currently operating in China voice the same complaints expressed by USTR in its report to Congress. In particular, U.S. and other foreign banks reportedly are concerned that restrictions on their ability to access renminbi-denominated deposits will make it difficult to meet the loans-to-deposit ratio requirement.[46] In an interview with CRS, an officer for one U.S. bank claimed that Chinese regulators are requiring U.S. banks to open a branch in a commercially undesirable city in order to obtain approval for a branch in a more commercially desirable city. U.S. banks also indicate that they are facing stiffer competition from Chinese commercial banks, who seemingly face fewer barriers to opening new branches or expanding operations.

Despite the perceived problems, some U.S. banks reportedly plan to expand their operations in China. Citigroup announced in December 2010 that it plans to have about 100

> **U.S. WTO Case Against China on Electronic Payment Services**
>
> On September 15, 2010, USTR filed a case against China for excluding U.S. suppliers from China's electronic payment services market in violation of China's 2001 World Trade Organization accession agreement. In its press release announcing the filing of the case, USTR asserts that China had assured China Union Pay (CUP) of a monopoly for the handling of renminbi-denominated credit and debit card transactions. According to USTR, this monopoly violates Articles XVI and XVII of the General Agreement on Trade in Services (GATS), as well as provisions in China's WTO accession agreement. China denies it is violating either the GATS or its WTO accession agreement. The dispute (DS413) is currently before a WTO panel.
>
> In June 2010, CUP and Visa were involved in a dispute over the processing of their co-branded cards issued in China. Visa claims that, under the terms of their agreement, international transactions on co-branded cards must be processed on Visa's network. CUP counters that Visa does not have the right to prevent the transactions being processed on CUP's network or other networks.

branches in China within 2-3 years.[47] Citigroup has 31 branches in China. By comparison, China's largest lender, ICBC, has over 16,000 branches in China. According to sources in the banking industry, U.S. banks are especially interested in expanding into China's "second-tier" cities and providing financial services to China's growing middle class.[48]

Relationships Between Chinese Banks and the Central or Local Governments

An unresolved issue regarding Chinese banks is the extent to which regulatory reforms have led to the banks being operated on a commercial basis. One of the stated goals of China's banking

---

[46] "Foreign Lenders under Loan-to-Deposit Ratio Pressure," *Trading Markets*, December 27, 2010.

[47] Susan Li and Stephanie Tong, "Citigroup Targets 100 China Branches in 2-3 Years," *Bloomberg*, December 6, 2010.

[48] China has four super cities with the administrative status of provinces: Beijing, Chongqing, Shanghai, and Tianjin,. In the second administrative tier, below the four super cities, are the cities of Changchun, Chengdu, Dalian, Hangzhou, Harbin, Guangzhou, Ji'nan, Nanjing, Ningbo, Qingdao, Shenyang, Shenzhen, Wuhan, Xiamen, and Xi'an ...

reforms has been to transform the banks into relatively autonomous, profit-driven financial institutions, modeled to a certain extent after commercial banks in the United States and Western Europe. However, the relationships of the different types of banks in China with the central government and its various regulatory agencies, and with local government entities remain complex. While circumstances vary for each of the major types of Chinese banks, virtually all of them balance their commercial interests with the changing and sometimes conflicting directives and priorities issued by different arms of the central and local government. Below is a brief description of the operational patterns of the different types of Chinese banks and their relationships with government entities.

Policy Banks

China's three state-owned policy banks—the Agricultural Development Bank of China (ADBC), China Development Bank (CDB), and Export Import Bank of China (China Ex-Im Bank)—have been assigned specific functions in the nation's financial markets, much like Fannie Mae, Freddie Mac, and Ginnie Mae in the United States. The ADBC's main role is provide financial services to China's agricultural sector and its rural population. The CDB's primary function is to finance major development projects, particularly infrastructure projects. The core function of the China Ex-Im Bank, as its name implies, is to help finance China's imports and exports.

China's policy banks operate financially by either receiving a capital contribution from the central government or by issuing bonds to raise capital. Because the bonds are issued by a policy bank, they are presumed to be backed by the full faith and credit of the Chinese government, with little or no risk of non-payment. This allows the policy banks to raise capital at a reduced cost. Once they have the necessary capital, the policy banks then provide loans or lines of credit to finance projects designated by bank management.

The annual reports of two of the three policy banks seem to emphasize their role in implementing the policies set by China's State Council. President Zheng Hui of the Agricultural Development Bank of China (ADBC) wrote in his bank's 2010 annual report that the bank, "produced fruitful business results by conscientiously implementing China's major policies in terms of economy and finance, as well as 'three rural issues' (agriculture, farmer and rural area issues) and continuing to strengthen the credit support for agriculture."[49] In China Ex-Im Bank's 2010 annual report, bank president Li Ruogu wrote of "the completion of our targets under the Eleventh Five-year Plan," including helping launch the State Council's regional development strategy and the revitalization of China's shipbuilding industry.[50]

The lending practices of the ADBC and China Ex-Im Bank also reflect their stipulated economic roles. Virtually all of ADBC's 1.67 trillion yuan in loans in 2010 went to providing credit for agricultural production, including 923.6 billion yuan (55.3%) in loans to purchase grain and edible oils. Similarly, most of China Ex-Im Bank's business activities in 2010 were trade-related transactions consistent with its specified function and the directives of the central government. However, both banks reported on their efforts to improve their risk management system and

---

[49] Agricultural Development Bank of China, *2010 Annual Report*, 2011, http://www.adbc.com.cn/report/2010report/en/2 htm.

[50] Export Import Bank of China, *Annual Report 2010*, 2011, http://english.eximbank.gov.cn/annual/2010.shtml.

reduce their levels of non-performing loans (NPLs), demonstrating a concern about the bank's overall profitability and solvency.[51]

China's third policy bank—China Development Bank (CDB)—faces a different situation than ADBC and China Ex-Im Bank. CDB has been scheduled for equitization since 2007, but has intentionally resisted its transformation. Over the last four years, CDB Chairman Chen Yuan (the eldest son of one of China's most famous economists, the late Chen Yun) has purposely forestalled CDB's equitization while at the same time expanding the bank's activities well beyond the policy role of financing China's major development projects. Under Chen's leadership, CDB has become one of China's more dynamic banks, operating like a commercial banks when it serves its purpose, and benefitting from its status as a policy bank when that is to its advantage.[52]

CDB's original mission was to finance large-scale infrastructure and industrial projects by providing long-term loans and lines of credit. CDB was a major source of credit for China's Three Gorges hydroelectric project and the nation's high-speed railway system. According to its 2010 annual report, 73.7% of its new loans—422 billion yuan ($66.4 billion)—in 2010 went to key sectors, such as coal, electricity, oil, telecommunications, transportation and public infrastructure.[53] Based on these figures, CDB would appear to be much like the other two policy banks.

However, a closer examination of CDB's lending activities reveals evidence that it has broadened its operations well beyond its prescribed policy role.[54] Two of the more important innovations promoted by Chen are providing credit for domestic projects collateralized by local government investment corporations (LICs) and supplying loans for international investments by state-owned enterprises (SOEs), particularly energy and natural resources investments. The domestic investments are notable because of the innovative means for securing the loans. The international loans are important because they have helped finance China's early effort to encourage its firms to go global.

CDB was the first major Chinese bank to finance local infrastructure projects by means of LICs. Under Chinese law, local governments cannot currently issue bonds or borrow from banks to finance infrastructure projects.[55] However, an LIC can. Under the arrangement developed by CDB, the local government authorizes an LIC to develop a parcel of land. The LIC, in turn, uses the value of the land to collateralize a loan from CDB to finance a project. In theory, the sale of the completed commercial or residential property development, or the proceeds from the operation of the infrastructure project are sufficient to service the debt. Based on CDBs success, many Chinese commercial banks entered into loan arrangements with LICs. According to one study, the cumulative value of LIC borrowing at the end of 2009 was 11.4 trillion yuan, or more

---

[51] For more on the risk management priorities of ADBC and China Ex-Im Bank, see http://www.adbc.com.cn/report/ 2010report/en/11 htm and http://english.eximbank.gov.cn/annual/2010/2010nb42-43.pdf

[52] For more about the transformation of CDB, see Erica Downs, *Inside China, Inc.: China Development Bank's Cross-Border Energy Deals*, Brooking Institution, John L. Thornton China Center Monograph Series, Number 3, March 2011.

[53] China Development Bank, *2010 Annual Report*, 2011, http://www.cdb.com.cn/english/Column.asp?ColumnId=91.

[54] For a more detailed examination of CDB's lending activities, see Erica Downs, *Inside China, Inc.: China Development Bank's Cross-Border Energy Deals*, Brooking Institution, John L. Thornton China Center Monograph Series, Number 3, March 2011.

[55] A draft revision to China's Budget Law would change that. China's unicameral legislature, the National People's Congress, had been expected to review the draft language in August 2011, but its review was postponed and no new date has been set.

---

than one-third of China's gross domestic product.[56] As will be discussed below, this innovative financial arrangement has raised some concern about the strength of China's commercial banks, given the comparatively high prices of real estate in China, and the perceived risk of a property bubble.

CDB was also one of the first and most aggressive banks to take advantage of the China's "Going Out" strategy (走出去战略) adopted at the 16th National Congress of the Chinese Communist Party in November 2002.[57] In 2003, CDB provided a major state-owned corporation, Sinochem, with a $230 million line of credit so it could acquire Atlantis, a subsidiary of Norwegian Petroleum Geo-Service (PGS). CDB subsequently worked out an arrangement with the National Development and Reform Commission (NDRC), a super-ministry under the State Council, whereby the two entities will draft an annual plan for overseas projects to be financed by CDB. Under the arrangement, CDB will independently assess the proposed projects and negotiate the terms of the loans. By 2009, CDB's overseas loans had grown to nearly $100 billion, representing 17% of the bank's outstanding loans.[58]

CDB's overseas activities have not been limited to loans to Chinese energy companies. In 2007, CDB was designated by the State Council to be the financier for the newly established China – Africa Development Fund. According to the Chinese government, the Fund was established to promote economic cooperation between China and Africa, and advance Africa's economic development. Critics of the Fund, however, maintain that it has been used by the Chinese government to secure access to important energy and mineral resources, while providing limited developmental benefit to the African countries involved.[59]

CDB's relationships with China's central government, as well as with the companies to which CDB has lent money, have become a balance between the different interests of the involved entities. In the words of a recent study of CDB's energy-backed loans (EBLs):[60]

> Although many media reports on the EBLs portrayed them as the quest of a monolithic China to secure oil and natural gas supplies, the reality is that these transactions involved multiple actors and a complex mix of motivations. First, the deals supported CDB's agenda, which included growing profits, demonstrating that China still needs CDB to function as a policy bank, ... and expanding the bank's international business. Second, the EBL's advanced the State Council's goals of enhancing China's access to energy and diversifying China's foreign exchange reserves. Third, CDB's loans helped China's NOCs [national oil companies] further their objective of acquiring exploration and production assets abroad.

For its own part, CDB has demonstrated an ability to operate with some autonomy, while remaining a wholly state-owned policy bank.

---

[56] Victor Shih, :Big Rock Candy Mountain," *China Economic Quarterly*, June 2010, pp. 26-32.

[57] The "Going Out" strategy involves increasing outward foreign direct investment, expanding product diversification, developing overseas brand recognition for Chinese goods, and offering new financial channels for overseas projects and investments.

[58] Downs, pg. 25.

[59] For more about the China –Africa Development Fund, see D. Marko Cimbaljevich, "China's New Safari into African Development," *Foreign Policy Digest*, May 1, 2010.

[60] Erica Downs, *Inside China, Inc.: China Development Bank's Cross-Border Energy Deals*, Brooking Institution, John L. Thornton China Center Monograph Series, Number 3, March 2011, p. 61.

Equitized Banks

Following their transformation from state-owned policy banks to joint-stock companies, China's five equitized banks no longer had access to direct capital allotments from the central government or the ability to issue no-risk, government-backed bonds to raise capital. Instead, they were expected to operate like commercial banks, drawing in deposits and dispensing loans to cover expenses and possibly earn a profit. The banks also were able to raise capital via their initial public offering (IPO) of stock. However, the central government was unwilling to fully relinquish control over the equitized banks. Banking regulations continue to restrict the types of financial services they can provide, the amount of credit they can extend, the interest rates they can charge, and other aspects of the banks' operations.

The 2010 annual reports of the five equitized banks reveal some important aspects of their financial operations (see **Table 6**) as of the end of 2010. The largest assets for all five banks were loans, with the value of corporate loans three or more times the value of personal loans. The personal loans provided by the five equitized banks were predominately mortgage loans. The banks' assets included significant investments in securities and other financial assets, which includes holdings of government and corporate bonds. The banks also maintained significant balances with other financial institutions—including their required reserves at the PBOC. On the liability side, customer deposits—both corporate and personal—dominated the balance sheets of the five equitized banks. Customer deposits were at least three-quarters of each of the bank's liabilities, but the relative proportion of corporate and personal deposits varied from bank to bank. Based on their balance sheets, China's equitized banks in 2010 were—like most commercial banks—taking in deposits from corporations, individuals and other entities, and recycling the funds as loans to corporations and individuals, as well as investments in securities and other assets (see **Table 6**).

Table 6. Simplified Balance Sheets for Five Equitized Banks

As of December 31, 2010, in trillion yuan

	Agricultural Bank of China	Bank of China	Bank of Communications	China Construction Bank	Industrial and Commercial Bank of China
Total Assets	10.337	10.460	3.952	10.810	13.459
- Loans	4.617	5.661	2.237	5.669	6.791
- Corporate Loans	3.378	4.144	1.819	3.977	4.700
- Personal Loans	1.001	1.416	0.418	1.369	1.633
- Investments in Securities and Other Financial Assets	2.527	2.055	0.810	2.905	3.732
- Cash and Balances with Other Banks	2.082	2.375	0.850	1.990	2.532
Liabilities	9.795	9.784	3.728	10.109	12.637
- Deposits from Customers	8.888	7.483	2.868	9.075	11.146
- Corporate Deposits	3.533	3.985	1.955	4.948	5.471

	Agricultural Bank of China	Bank of China	Bank of Communications	China Construction Bank	Industrial and Commercial Bank of China
- Personal Deposits	5.065	3.453	0.906	4.023	5.244
- Deposits from Other Financial Institutions	0.583	1.580	0.717	0.750	1.048
New Worth	0.542	0.676	0.224	0.701	0.822

Source: 2010 annual reports of each bank

The five equitized banks apparently were fairly successful in their operations in 2010. The Agricultural Bank of China (ABC) reported net profits of 94.9 billion yuan ($14.9 billion) in 2010. Bank of China (BOC) reported net profits of 9.7 billion yuan ($1.5 billion). The reported net profit for the Bank of Communications was 39.0 billion yuan ($6.1 billion). China Construction Bank (CCB) reported 134.8 billion yuan ($21.2 billion) in net profit in 2010, while the Industrial and Commercial Bank of China (ICBC) reported net profit for 2010 of 166.0 billion ($26.1 billion). A recent study of equitized Chinese banks determined that "post-listing earning figures are consistent with banks adopting a more market-driven orientation."[61]

Despite the partial privatization of the equitized banks, some observers maintain that China's central government continues to exert a strong influence over the lending practices and administration of these banks via various means.[62] First, the board of directors of the banks and the senior bank officers are generally directly appointed by the Communist Party Organization Department, and usually come from central government or Party agencies or one of the equitized banks.[63] Second, the career opportunities for senior bank officers largely depend on the assessments of the official agencies responsible for their appointment, which according to some observers, make them more responsive to the wishes of the central government than to the interests of the shareholders of the bank. Third, according to some accounts, the central government agencies will apply direct pressure on the bank officials to provide loans and services to specific projects or investments.

In interviews with CRS, officials of China's equitized banks described the operation of their banks and, in particular, their lending practices. The officials reported that the banks have established modern risk assessment procedures to assess prospective clients and strive to operate on a commercial basis. However, they also noted that the PBOC and CBRC apply pressure on bank officials to adjust their lending practices to conform with government policy priorities, such as providing greater assistance to small- and medium-sized enterprises (SMEs), or slowing the growth rate of credit in China. None of the officials interviewed mentioned being pressured to provide a specific loan to a specific company.

---

[61] Paul B. McGuinness and Kevin Keasey, "The Listing of Chinese State-Owned Banks and their Path to Banking and Ownership Reform," *China Quarterly*, vol. 201 (March 2010), p. 145.

[62] One example of this argument is "Privatisation in China: Capitalism Confined," *Economist*, September 3, 2011.

[63] For example, BOC's non-executive directors include individuals from PBOC, SAFE, and the Treasury Bureau. Prior to coming to BOC, the bank's executive directors either worked at another equitized banks or PBOC.

However, the bank officials did say that their banks' past relations with state-owned and larger private companies when the banks were still policy banks did influence their lending patterns. According to the bank officials, the banks perceive their past creditors more favorably than new creditors, and the banks have a tendency to provide loans to the larger, well-established state-owned and private corporations.

Some of the bank officials commented on a dilemma they faced in 2008 when China's central government was trying to stimulate the economy by pumping more credit into the market. The PBOC and other government officials pressured the equitized banks to provide more loans to SMES, rather than larger companies, as this would supposedly create more jobs and be subject to less public criticism. During the same time, the CBRC reminded banks about the dangers of non-performing loans (NPLs) and cautioned the banks about offering credit to riskier companies. Because the equitized banks generally perceive SMEs as higher risk than larger companies which have a credit history with the bank, the bank officials said that the banks generally resisted the pressures from the government to lend to SMEs during the financial crisis.

The dynamic between the central government and the five equitized banks appears to be very similar to the relationship between CDB and the central government described above. The equitized banks seem to be striving to balance the goals of the bank to earn profits and expand operations with the overall economic policy objectives stipulated by the State Council, PBOC, and other government entities. In addition, the equitized banks also take into consideration the financial needs of their major clients—China's SOEs and larger private corporations—to insure repayment of their outstanding loans and maintain good relations with increasingly influential figures in China's political system.[64]

City Commercial Banks

The city commercial banks primarily interact with the Chinese government at the provincial or municipal level, but are still supervised by the PBOC and the CBRC. Like the equitized banks, the city commercial banks have been largely transformed into private joint stock companies, with shares owned by local government agencies, investment companies and other legal entities, and individual investors (see **Table 7**). In addition, the officers of the city commercial banks generally are also shareholders.

---

[64] For more about the role of SOEs and private corporations in Chinese political system, see CRS Report R41007, *Understanding China's Political System* , by Michael F. Martin.

Table 7. Sample Shareholding Structure of City Commercial Banks

In percentage of outstanding shares

	Government Owned	Legal Entities	Individuals (including Bank Officers)	Bank Officers
Bank of Chongqing	53.9	43.2	2.8	1.7
Fujian Haixia Bank	29.9	49.9	20.2	0.6
Guangxi Beibu Gulf Bank	28.7	68.2	0.7	n.a.
Hankou Bank	3.7	91.9	4.4	0.2
Harbin Bank	33.7	61.2	5.1	n.a.

Source: 2010 annual reports (in Chinese) of each bank, available online

Notes: Legal entities includes investment companies, banks and other corporations which may or may not be wholly or partially owned by government agencies.

In many cases, share ownership is concentrated among a small set of shareholders. For the five city commercial banks listed in **Table 7**, the top 10 shareholders in 2010 held between 46.0% and 90.2% of the banks' shares. Many of the top 10 shareholders were investment companies associated with corporations, such as trading companies, railroads, power companies, and telecommunications companies. A few local government agencies were also on the top 10 investor lists, such as the finance departments of Fuzhou City and Wuhan City. Among the top 10 shareholders in the Bank of Chongqing was Dah Sing Bank of Hong Kong.

Like the equitized banks, the city commercial banks generally have a board of directors and appointed bank officers responsible for the operation of the bank. The board of directors of city commercial banks generally include senior officials from the major shareholders, including representatives from government agencies. Many of the board members have experience working for banks, while some have also worked for local governments. Similarly, the bank officers usually have experience working for banks or for local governments. The apparent close ties between the city commercial bank officials and local government officials would support the idea that the banks are highly responsive to the preferences of local governments.

The financial statements of the city commercial banks reflect their smaller size and their lower reliance on loans (see **Table 8**). The five city commercial banks had total assets about 1% the size of those of the equitized banks. They also relied more on various forms of investments, including a high volume of reverse repurchase agreements. The reverse repurchase agreements are effectively a form of securitized loan, in which the bank temporarily acquires title to an asset from the borrower, who promises to repurchase the assets at a higher price at a future date. The difference between the bank's acquisition price and the borrower's repurchase price provides the return to the bank. The city commercial banks had comparatively low levels of personal deposits when compared to the five equitized banks (see **Table 6** and **Table 8**).

Table 8. Simplified Balance Sheet for City Commercial Banks

As of December 31, 2010; in billion yuan

	Bank of Chongqing	Fujian Haixia Bank	Guangxi Beibu Gulf Bank	Hankou Bank	Harbin Bank
Total Assets	108.239	53.368	59.228	111.766	127.170
- Loans	51.955	23.693	17.018	36.966	54.025
- Corporate Loans	36.027[a]	14.191	14.201	32.999	30.356
- Personal Loans	5.018[a]	7.284	3.188	4.707	23.668
- Investments in Securities and Other Financial Assets	37.089	19.785	30.230	40.600	36.113
- Reverse Repayment Agreements	15.584	7.656	25.025	9.764	17.863
- Cash and Balances with Other Banks	15.065	6.613	7.048	12.646	32.861
Liabilities	103.248	48.902	55.062	105.288	121.926
- Deposits from Customers	73.856	37.776	34.336	85.616	112.892
- Corporate Deposits	58.043[a]	25.788	25.627	55.495	79.832
- Personal Deposits	10.831[a]	5.391	6.217	20.346	32.051
- Deposits from Other Financial Institutions	1.310	1.339	1.292	0.028	0.170
New Worth	4.991	4.467	4.167	6.478	14.278

Source: 2010 annual reports (in Chinese) of banks, available online

Notes: Columns may not balance due to rounding error and omission of additional categories.

a.   Figures show daily average balance; not year-end amount.

The city commercial banks appear to remain tied financially to their region, with a focus on serving the needs of the local business community. The leading borrowers in 2010 for the five selected banks were almost exclusively from the city or province in which the banks are located, according to their annual reports. While details of top depositors were not provided in the annual report, it is likely that most of them are also from the bank's home city or province. Only Harbin Bank has developed a considerable personal loan portfolio, and most of that lending is for mortgages. However, some city commercial banks (such as Bank of Beijing, Bank of Shanghai, and Bank of Tianjin) have been allowed by the CBRC to open branches outside of their home city or province, indicating an interest on the part of some banks and the banking regulators to see the city commercial banks develop beyond their traditional regional role.

The current institutional arrangements would appear to place the officers of China's city commercial banks in a sometimes difficult and confining situation. The banks' shareholders, including some of the larger corporations in the region and local government agencies, may push for higher profits and greater returns on their investments, but at the same time, seek preferential treatment for their loan requests and deposits at the banks. In addition, the central government and its regulatory agencies may encourage the banks to direct their financial services towards providing greater support for certain types of customers or lending activities. In many respects, the city commercial banks face a similar situation as the other types of banks discussed previously, with the additional complexity of addressing the desires of local government entities and local corporate shareholders.

Joint-Stock Commercial Banks

China's joint-stock commercial banks have a mixture of ownership structures (see **Table 9**). The 12 banks were established as commercial banks after China began its economic reforms, and were subsequently transformed into joint-stock companies. In most cases, the original state entities that owned the bank remained a major stock holder after the conversion, but were allowed to divest their shares after a mandatory holding period. For some banks, the state-owned entity chose to remain a major shareholder (for example, CITIC Bank). For at least 10 of the 12 banks, a foreign entity has purchased a significant holding of the outstanding shares, often after the bank received permission to list H shares on the Hong Kong stock exchange, the Hong Kong Exchanges and Clearing Limited, or HKEx (see **Table 9**).

Table 9. Shareholdings of China's Private Banks

As of December 31, 2010

Bank	Percentage of Shares Held by State or State-owned Entity	Percentage of Shares Held by Non-state Domestic Entities	Percentage of Shares Held by Foreign Entities	Major Domestic Shareholder	Major Foreign Shareholder
China Bohai Bank	62.01	18.00	19.99	Tianjin TEDA Investment Holding Co.	Standard Chartered Bank (HK)
China Everbright Bank	74.04	21.61	4.35	Central Huijin Investment Co.	China Everbright Ltd. (HK)
China Merchants Bank	At least 35.3	Not stated	At least 17.83	China Merchants Steam Navigation Co.	JPMorgan Chase & Co. (USA)
China Minsheng Bank	Not stated	At least 26.91	At least 15.27	New Hope Investment Co.	Morgan Stanley & Co. (USA)
China Zheshang Bank	At least 14.29	Not stated	Not stated	Zhejiang Province Financial Services Development Co.	Not stated
CITIC Bank	At least 63.08	Not Stated	At least 30.82	CITIC Group	BBVA (Spain)
Evergrowing Bank	Not stated	Not stated	At least 8.33	Yantai Blue Sky Investment Holding Co.	Daiwa Bank (Singapore)
Guangdong Development Bank	72.20	4.11	23.69	China Life Insurance Co.	Citigroup (USA)
Huaxia Bank	At least 35.99%	At least 6.65	At least 17.12	Shougang Corp.	Deutsche Bank (Germany)

Bank	Percentage of Shares Held by State or State-owned Entity	Percentage of Shares Held by Non-state Domestic Entities	Percentage of Shares Held by Foreign Entities	Major Domestic Shareholder	Major Foreign Shareholder
Industrial Bank	At least 28.89	At least 3.64%	At least 12.80	Finance Bureau of Fujian Province	Hang Seng Bank (HK)
Shanghai Pudong Bank	Not stated	Not stated	At least 2.71	China Mobile Ltd.	Citibank (USA)
Shenzhen Development Bank	Not stated	Not stated	Not stated	Ping An Insurance Group Ltd.	Not stated

Source: 2010 annual reports of each bank

Notes: Data for Evergrowing Bank is for 2009; 2010 annual report not available.

The number of actual shareholders for the 12 banks also varied. At one extreme, China Bohai Bank had only seven shareholders as of the end of 2010. At the other extreme, China Minsheng Bank reported 1,123,423 shareholders as of December 31, 2010. In most cases, the major shareholders have at least one representative on the bank's board of directors. In contrast to the city commercial banks, the senior management of the joint-stock commercial banks generally are not shareholders. The senior officers of the private banks are appointed by the board of directors; most of the senior officers have a career working in the banking sector.

Based on their balance sheets, China's joint-stock commercial banks show some similarities to the city commercial banks (see **Table 10**). Loans are the largest assets for all 12 banks, but they the banks generally also have significant holdings of reverse repurchase agreements. In addition, deposits dominate the banks' liabilities. For five of the banks, deposits constitute more than three-quarters of their liabilities.

From their management structures, stock ownership and balance sheets, it can be inferred that China's joint-stock commercial banks are largely operating on a commercial basis, but may face pressure from two distinct quarters to allocate loans and resources at variance with optimal business practices. First, the continued presence of the local government or government-owned entities as major shareholders – often with a voting member on the bank's board of directors – provides the local governments with direct and indirect means to influence the operation of the banks. Second, the banks may also be under pressure from private stockholders who also have a voting member on the board – including their overseas investors – to provide preferential treatment to their companies, their families, and/or their friends.

Table 10. Simplified Balance Sheets for China's Joint-Stock Commercial Banks

As of December 31, 2010

Banks	Portion of Assets Held As:		Portion of Liabilities Held as Deposits
	Loans and Advances	Reverse Repurchase Agreements	
China Bohai Bank	34.3%	35.4%	50.7%
China Everbright Bank	51.4%	11.5%	73.6%
China Merchants Bank	58.4%	n.a.	79.0%
China Minsheng Bank	56.9%	n.a.	77.7%
China Zheshang Bank	51.2%	10.6%	72.2%
CITIC Bank	59.9%	7.1%	83.2%
Evergrowing Bank	43.5%	13.5%	62.4%
Guangdong Development Bank	55.4%	16.8%	77.0%
Huaxia Bank	49.5%	23.1%	73.8%
Industrial Bank	45.6%	20.2%	61.2%
Shanghai Pudong Bank	51.3%	17.9%	74.8%
Shenzhen Development Bank	55.1%	13.5%	77.4%

Source: 2010 annual reports of banks

Notes: Data for Evergrowing Bank is for 2009; 2010 annual report not available.

Government Run or Not?

All of China's banks share a common governance system, involving senior bank officers, a board of directors, and a board of supervisors. The senior bank officers are members of the Chinese Communist Party (CCP) and are appointed by the CCP. The officers are also assigned ranks in the Chinese government's hierarchy, ranging from the equivalent of a bureau chief to a vice-minister.[65] The professional careers of the senior bank officers is determined by the CCP, and may involve moving into positions within the Party, the central or local governments, or other banks depending on the officer's performance. For example, In November 2011, Wang Hongzhan, previously PBOC's deputy governor was appointed as CCB's chairman and Party secretary, replacing Guo Shuqing, who was appointed chairman of the China Securities Regulatory Commission.[66]

The Board of Directors consist of a mix of senior bank officials, persons appointed by major shareholders, and supposedly "independent directors (独立董事)." However, some of the "independent directors" are also senior officials in governmental financial agencies or with other financial institutions. In a few cases, some of the "independent directors" are foreign nationals.

---

[65] For more details about the significance of China's government ranking system, see CRS Report R41007, *Understanding China's Political System*, by Michael F. Martin.

[66] Wen Xiu, "Bank Sector Execs Follow the Revolving Door," *Caixin*, December 6, 2011.

The main responsibilities of the board of directors of Chinese banks, much like for U.S. banks, is to oversee the activities of the senior bank officials and the set general policies of the bank.

The board of supervisors usually include individuals appointed by the CCP, the bank's labor union, the major shareholders, and "external supervisors" (外部监事) who frequently have positions with some other entity involved in China's financial system. The board of supervisors for Chinese banks monitor the financial activity, risk management and risk control of the bank as well as the performance of the board of directors and the senior officials of the bank.

Some commentators on China's banking system explicitly or implicitly maintain that China's banks continue to operate as direct tools of the Chinese government. In this view, the government-appointed bank officers distribute loans and credit in accordance with directives of the State Council or its agents – the Ministry of Finance, the PBOC, or the CBRC. Additional evidence used to demonstrate the continued interference of the central government in the operations of China's bank are the allocation of credit limits, the regulation of interest rates, and anecdotal accounts of banks being instructed to provide credit to selected businesses as part of a larger national or provincial economic policy.

Other commentators maintain this view oversimplifies the operational situation for Chinese banks and fails to appreciate recent developments. While the PBOC continues to set overall credit growth targets for the year, it no longer allocates credit limits to individual banks. It is relying on changes in the reserve requirement and interest rates to control the money supply. Also, banks have more latitude than in the past in setting interest rates on loans; the PBOC still sets base interest rates for different types of loans, but interest rate ceilings have been eliminated. In addition, bank managers are reportedly using creative means to bend or evade regulations designed to curtail or redirect credit allocations.[67]

Although China's central and local governments continue to wield significant influence over the operations of China's banks, these commentators say, they are no longer simply extensions of the government. Through business relations with foreign banks, most Chinese banks have established modern risk management systems and strive to allocate their resources based on commercial criteria. However, the Chinese banks are constrained by various circumstances that periodically require that the banks acquiesce to external pressures. The central government at times will pressure the banks to align their credit allocation along with national economic policy. Local governments may lobby the banks to extend loans to preferred local companies. Overseas investors and companies that are major shareholders may also seek preferential treatment for certain projects or companies. Sometimes, these pressures may contradict each other, placing the bank managers in a bind. Despite these constraints and others, China's banks have to a significant extent substantially shifted over to a commercially-based business model.

The CBRC appears to be dissatisfied with the incomplete transition of bank management to a commercially-based business model. It has drafted a "consultative document" for additional reforms of the governance of China's commercial banks. The "Guidelines for Corporate Governance of Commercial Banks" would apply to all commercial banks "that are approved by the banking supervisory authority to establish within the territory of [the] People's Republic of China."[68] Among the draft document's major provisions are:

---

[67] See Wen Xiu, "Bank Regulator's Loan Rules Appear Bendable," *Caixin*, August 15, 2011.

[68] China Banking Regulatory Commission, *Guidelines on Corporate Governance of Commercial Banks (Consultative* (continued...)

- A prohibition on shareholders interfering with decision-making and management of a bank;

- A ban on providing shareholders with preferential loans;

- Rules governing the nomination and election of directors and supervisors by shareholders, including limits on the number of candidates who can be nominated by individual shareholders and a requirement that shareholders vote on the nominees;

- Rules defining the duties of the board of directors, the board of supervisors, and the senior management of the bank;

- A requirement that the bank "support national policies on industrial transformation and environmental protection, protect and save resources, and promote the sustainable development of the society;"

- A requirement that the bank establish a "risk management department" and the delineation of the department's duties;

- A requirement that the bank use an external auditor;

- Requirements for the performance evaluation and compensation of directors, supervisors, and bank management; and

- Minimum standards for information disclosure.

In addition to the draft guidelines, the CBRC has issued notices, directives and guidelines designed to promote the management of banks based on risk/return assessments utilizing international best practices. These include a December 2010 guideline on performance appraisal for bank directors and a February 2010 guideline on compensation practices for bank employees, including top management.

Profitability and Solvency of Chinese Banks

The adoption of more commercially-based management has brought about the return of serious problems that were associated with China's banking system when it was under greater government control – non-performing loans (NPLs) and fears of insolvency. After several years of growing profitability and improved finances, China's banks appear to be poised for a rise in NPLs, particularly if there is a sharp decline in real estate values. Unresolved NPLs of the past, newly-emerging NPLs associated with a recent sharp rise in local government debt, and hidden exposure to underground banking have increased the likelihood that China's banks may experience a rise in NPLs and, in some cases, edge towards insolvency. While recent stress tests conducted by the CBRC indicate that most of the banks can survive a major drop in property prices, some banks – particularly city commercial banks – are more exposed. China's banking regulators have taken some steps to avoid a precipitous rise in NPLs. They are also discussing how to handle insolvent banks, if and when the issue arises.

(...continued)

Document), July 26, 2011.

The Legacy of China's 1999 Non-Performing Loans Write-Off

In 1999, China's banking system was virtually insolvent. Years of central government micromanagement of bank operations had resulted in the country's four major banks – ABC, BOC, CCB, and ICBC – drowning in a pool of NPLs. The precise extent of the problem was unknown, as the PBOC had dictated an upper limit on the percentage of loans that could be declared bad debt.[69] Besides the excessive interference by the central government, the major banks were in trouble because local governments and state-owned enterprises frequently defaulted on their loans, under the assumption that the central government would provide the necessary capital to keep the banks afloat.

As part of an effort to rescue the banking sector, the State Council transferred 1.4 trillion yuan in NPLs from the four major banks over to four newly created asset management companies (AMCs).[70] The NPLs of each bank were transferred to one of the new AMCs at full face value in 1999 and 2000 (see **Table 11**). According to some estimates, the initial transfer only represented about half of the NPLs held by the four banks, and did nothing to address the NPLs held by other Chinese banks. A second round of NPLs were transferred to the AMCs in 2004 and 2005, totaling a reported 1.6 trillion yuan.[71] In contrast to the 2000 transfer, the second round of NPLs were sold a discount on face value.[72] Additional transfers eventuallybrought the total NPL transfers from Chinese banks to the AMCs to nearly 3.6 trillion yuan ($566 billion).

Table 11. Non-Performing Loan Transfers of 1999-2000

Bank	Associated Asset Management Company (AMC)	Value of Non-Performing Loans Transferred	Share of Bank's Outstanding Loans
Agricultural Bank of China	China Great Wall AMC	345.8 billion yuan	24.6%
Bank of China	China Orient AMC	267.4 billion yuan	20.4%
China Construction Bank	China Cinda AMC	373.0 billion yuan[a]	21.7%
Industrial and Commercial Bank of China	China Huarong AMC	407.7 billion yuan	17.9%

Source: Ben Fung, Jason George, Stefan Hohl and Guonan Ma, "Public asset management companies in East Asia - Case studies," Financial Stability Institute - Occasional Paper No 3 Case Studies, February 2004.

Notes:

a. Includes 100 billion yuan of NPLs from China Development Bank.

---

[69] The PBOC stipulated that out of a bank's outstanding loans no more than 2% could be classified as "bad loans," 5% as "problem loans," and 8% as "loans of concern."

[70] According to Carl E. Walter and Fraser J.T. Howie, the AMCs were modeled after the Resolution Trust Corporation, which was established by the Financial Institutions Reform Recovery and Enforcement Act (FIRREA) of 1989 (P.L. 101-73) to handle the disposal of the assets of the collapsed U.S. savings and loans associations. See Carl E. Walter and Fraser J.T. Howie, *Red Capitalism: The Fragile Financial Foundation of China's Extraordinary Rise*, John Wiley & Sons, 2011 for more details about China's asset management companies.

[71] Carl E. Walter and Fraser J.T. Howie, *Red Capitalism: The Fragile Financial Foundation of China's Extraordinary Rise*, John Wiley & Sons, 2011.

[72] For example, China Cinda AMC purchased 278.7 billion in NPLs from BOC and CCB on June 21, 2004 at 30.98% of face value. (Alpha & Leader Law Firm, "Transactions Involving Non-performing Loans ("NPL") in China," August 2007.

The four AMCs were originally owned by the Ministry of Finance (MOF), and were instructed to attempt to recover as much of the debt as possible either by debt collection, debt restructuring, debt-equity swaps, or loan repackaging and resale. The AMCs were to be disbanded after 10 years. Each of the AMCs was provided 10 billion yuan ($1.6 billion) in initial capital by the Ministry of Finance in exchange for AMC bonds. In order to raise additional operating capital, the AMCs issued 858 billion yuan in bonds in 2000 with a coupon yield equal to the one-year deposit rate. The bonds were mostly bought by the four major banks, effectively bringing the NPLs back onto their books, but "disguised" as a new type of asset. In addition, the PBOC provided the AMCs with 634 billion yuan ($99.7 billion) in loans.

The AMCs used various means to attempt to recover the value of the NPLs. One of the main strategies was to bundle the bad loans by province, debtor, or industry and then sell the resulting loan portfolios to domestic and foreign investors. Among the U.S investors in the AMCs loan portfolios were Bank of America, BNY Mellon, Cargill, and Citigroup.

The asset recovery record for the AMCs through the first quarter of 2006 was below China's expectations of a 30% recovery rate. According to the CBRC, the four AMCs had disposed of 866.3 billion yuan ($136.2 billion) in loans, with a cash recovery of 180.6 billion yuan ($28.4 billion)(see **Table 12**). The resulting asset recovery rate was 24.2%, and the cash recovery rate was 20.8%. Based on the assumption that the easier-to-collect loans had been the first disposed of by the AMCs, China's banking officials decided to revisit the organization and operation of the AMCs.

The MOF decided to make two significant changes in the AMCs. First, the AMCs would be allowed to engage in a broader range of asset management activities, including purchasing share in other companies, as a means of providing them with more revenue. Second, the MOF sold minority interest in the AMCs to selected domestic investors. The Agricultural Bank of China acquired a 49% of China Great Wall AMC. China Construction Bank acquired 48% of China Cinda AMC. ICBC purchased 48% of China Huarong AMC. Bank of Communications obtained an unknown share of China Orient AMC. As a result, three of the four original major banks not only became large holders of dubious AMC bonds, they also became major equity owners in the possibly insolvent AMCs, raising questions about the underlying strength of the banks.

Table 12. Asset Recovery Results for Four AMCs

In billion yuan or percent

AMC	Value of Disposed NPLs	Cash Recovery	Asset Recovery Rate	Cash Recovery Rate
China Great Wall AMC	270.8	27.8	12.7%	10.3%
China Orient AMC	142.0	32.8	27.2%	23.1%
China Cinda AMC	206.8	65.3	34.5%	31.6%
China Huarong AMC	246.8	54.7	26.5%	22.2%

Source: China Banking Regulatory Commission, "Disposal of Non-performing assets by the four AMCs in 2006."

By 2008, the Chinese government's efforts to improve to underlying financial situation of its major banks had improved the appearance of the banks' balance sheets, but had seemingly done little to address the outstanding NPL problem. While a large portion of the banks' NPLs had been explicitly removed from the books of the banks, they had subsequently returned to their list of assets renamed as AMC bonds and investment holdings in the AMCs. The problem of unresolved loans remains an issue for China's banks.

Local Government Funding Platforms as a Possible Source of Non-Performing Loans

A second source of possible financial troubles for China's banks emerged out of the combined effects of China's post-global financial crisis stimulus program, flaws in local government financing, and the credit decisions of the banks. A new innovation in local finance called "local government funding platforms" is playing a central role in what may mature into a sharp rise in NPLs for China's banks.

The global financial crisis of 2008 seemed to catch China, and the rest of the world, off guard. To offset the sharp decline in global demand and the resulting slowdown in China's growth, the Chinese government announced in November 2008 a two-year, 4 trillion yuan ($629 billion) stimulus program designed to improve overall economic growth, invest in the nation's infrastructure, and stimulate domestic consumer demand.[73] According to the stimulus plan, 1.2 trillion yuan ($188 billion) of the funding would be provided by the central government; local governments would be responsible for 2.8 trillion yuan ($440 billion).

For the local governments, funding 70% of the stimulus program was a serious challenge. Local governments in China are limited in the ways by which they can raise revenues.[74] Local government cannot directly issue bonds. As a result, many local governments were unable to finance the stimulus program via regular means. Instead, they turned to an innovative method of raising revenues commonly known as "local government funding platforms."

The local government funding platforms involved the local government creating a separate incorporated entity for the purpose of financing the various local projects that were part of the national stimulus program. These entities, or "local investment companies" (LICs) – often given names using such words as "development" and "investment" – were given land use rights or development rights to designated locations by the local governments. The LICs would then use these rights to obtain loans from local banks or to issue bonds – which were often purchased by the local banks – to raise the necessary capital to develop the land or build the specified project. In some cases, the LICs resold the development rights to other companies. According to China's National Audit Office, 6,576 LICs had been created by June 2011 with a total debt of 4.97 trillion yuan ($782 billion).[75]

According to a survey by PBOC and CBRC, the local government funding platforms had borrowed 6 trillion yuan by September 2009, primarily from banks. The CBRC determined that 14% of new credit issued in China in 2009 was to local government funding platforms. The details of these loans varied, but in many cases, the underlying value of the land was used as collateral for the loans. In other cases, rather than provide loans, the banks apparently negotiated

---

[73] For more about China's stimulus program of 2008, see CRS Report RS22984, *China and the Global Financial Crisis: Implications for the United States*, by Wayne M. Morrison.

[74] In general, local governments are allocated a portion of personal income taxes, business taxes, and value-added taxes, plus levy property taxes, vehicle taxes, and various service charges.

[75] "China Debts Dwarf Official Data Too-Big-to-Finish Alarm," *Bloomberg*, December 19, 2011.

reverse repurchase agreements with the LICs. While an official breakdown is not available, it appears that city commercial banks and "private" banks were particularly active in providing credit to local government funding platforms.

At a national level, it appears that China's credit market was unable to effectively absorb the national stimulus program. While much of the funding went to infrastructure construction and other useful development projects, a significant portion of the funds was used by local companies to purchase stocks on China's stock market and make real estate investments. As a consequence, property values in many Chinese cities rose dramatically. This, in turn, led to inflated real estate prices, which raised the amount of credit made available by banks to local government funding platforms.

The possible excessive provision and misallocation may have been exacerbated by central government pressures on local banks to provide more credit to small and medium-sized enterprises. The initial reaction of bank managers to the stimulus program reportedly was to offer more credit to its more reliable customers, which were usually larger state-owned enterprises.[76] Subsequently, the PBOC indicated that the banks should make sure that other customers received a reasonable portion of the stimulus credit. According to some accounts, the banks' credit officers lacked the experience or the resources to adequately assess the risk associated with the large volume of loans being approved. The threat of rising NPLs appeared to be mounting.

The Risks of Underground Banking

In the fall of 2011, the City of Wenzhou in Zhejiang Province, nationally known as the birthplace of the model for the development of private enterprise in China during the 1980s and a major high-speed rail crash in July 2011, once again captured national attention as dozens of private entrepreneurs closed their factories, stores, and businesses, and fled town to escape their creditors.[77] Despite strong sales and factory orders, the business owners faced financial ruin because of their inability to service loans secured via the city's "underground banks." By October 5, the crisis was so severe that Premier Wen Jiabao and PBOC Governor Zhou Xiaochuan visited the city to discuss ways of preventing any spread of the financial instability.

The Wenzhou financial crisis exposed a previously unseen and underappreciated vulnerability in China's banking system. Unable to obtain loans from China's banks, private companies in Wenzhou and across the country had turned to "underground banks" to obtain their desired credit. Estimates of the size of the "underground" loan market vary, ranging up to 4 trillion yuan ($630 billion).[78] The credit, however, came at a high cost; interest rates for "underground bank" loans reportedly ran as high as 180% in some cases.[79] A spokesperson for the CBRC, however, estimated that underground interest rates varies from 14% to 70%.[80] By comparison, Chinese banks at the time were offering lending rates between 7% and 8% for commercial loans.[81] A

---

[76] Andrew Batson and Jason Leow, "China Credit Boom Spurs Concern - Officials Weigh More Regulation, Fearing Banks are Taking on Too Much Risk," *Wall Street Journal*, April 21, 2009.

[77] Olivia Chung, "China's Debt-Heavy Bosses Go on the Run," *Asia Times*, October 1, 2011.

[78] "China to Control Shadow Banking and Private Lending," *BBC*, October 19, 2011.

[79] Ma Guangyuan, "What Do We Have for Wenzhou's Rescue," *China-US Focus*, November 16, 2011.

[80] "China to Control Shadow Banking and Private Lending," *BBC-*, October 19, 2011.

[81] Zhang Bing, Zheng Fei, and Zhao Jingting, "Cash Crash for Wenzhou's Private Loan Network," *Caixin*, October 11, 2011.

survey by the PBOC branch in Wenzhou revealed that 89% of Wenzhou households and 60% of the local businesses were involved in underground banking in some form.[82]

The largely unregulated and unmonitored "underground banks" had grown rapidly prior to the outbreak of the Wenzhou financial crisis for several reasons. The strict ceilings on interest rates for deposit accounts had provided an incentive for some people and businesses to seek higher rates of return for their cash holdings. The tightening of monetary policy which followed China's post-global financial crisis stimulus package had reduced the amount of credit Chinese banks could offer. Rising prices for real estates and stocks stimulated speculative behavior by individual investors and commercial businesses.

Seemingly unbeknownst to China's banks and its financial regulators, businesses took cash obtained from commercial loans with banks and lent it to private businesses and individuals – who in turn, sometime lent the money to other businesses and individuals – at the higher "underground" interest rates. Some reports say that government officials and bank officers also participated in underground lending, using their positions to obtain loans from the banks.[83] This created the mechanism whereby the collapse of the underground banks of Wenzhou threatened to spread to China's banking system. It is believed that much of the money raised by underground loans was invested in real estate and the stock market. When prices for real estate and stocks stopped their rapid ascent, the creditors defaulted on their "underground' loans. No longer receiving payments on the credit they had provided in underground loans, many of the holders of the commercial bank loans were unable to service their debt and the Chinese banks saw a rise in the NPL rates.

As Wenzhou's financial crisis subsided (see **Government Response to Non-performing Loan Concerns** below), concerns about underground banking receded in the news. The issue reemerged just prior to Chinese New Years, a time when people traditionally attempt to settle all their debts. China Daily published a special weekly supplement in early January that included multiple stories on underground banking, the credit crunch for private enterprises, and the government's response to these economic problems.[84] The supplement's lead story portrays a mixed picture of the underground banking situation, with some commentators worried that a new crisis could emerged and critical of the government's response, and other commentators maintaining that efforts to provide private enterprises with credit and improved oversight will prevent a reoccurrence of the events in Wenzhou.[85]

Government Response to Non-performing Loan Concerns

The CBRC was the first government agency to perceive the possible risk associated with the surge in credit accompanying the stimulus program and the emergence of local government funding platforms. In March 2009, the CBRC warned China's banks and local governments about the possible rise of NPLs. In the spring of 2009, the CBRC required China's commercial banks to review their loans to local government funding platforms and restructure them as necessary to

---

[82] Ibid.

[83] Ibid.

[84] "USA Weekly," *China Daily*, January 6-12, 2012.

[85] "Credit Crunch," *China Daily (USA Weekly)*, January 6-12, 2012.

reduce the risk on non-payment. In addition, the CBRC conducted a stress test study of China's banks to determine if they could withstand a sharp decline in property values.

The CBRC's initial stress test conducted in 2009 considered the impact of a 30% decline in property values on the financial health of the banks.[86] According to the study, a 30% decline would increase the NPL rate by 2.2% and the bank's pre-tax profits would decline by 20%. In general, the banks would survive the market decline. In April 2011, the CRBC ordered the banks to conduct a subsequent stress test examining the effects of a 50-60% drop in property values. The results of the second set of stress tests have not been released, but CBRC Chairman Liu Mingkang said in October 2011 that China's banks could sustain a 40% price drop in the real estate market.[87]

In addition to conducting stress tests, the CBRC has introduced new requirements for the management of Chinese banks' lending practices. The new requirements – collectively known as the "Three Rules and One Guideline" – consist of:

- Provisional Rules on the Management of Fixed Assets;

- Provisional Rules on the Management of Working Capital;

- Provisional Rules on the Management of Retail Loans; and

- Guidelines on Project Financing.

According to CBRC, the "Three Rules and One Guideline" are designed to tighten loan management by controlling the dispersal of credit until the funds are to be used, providing credit only to the extent needed by the borrower, strengthening loan contract enforcement, and maintaining supervision of the loan throughout the lending process.[88]

In a reported effort to provide local governments with a new way to raise funds, the State Council approved a pilot program allowing Guangdong Province, Shanghai Municipality, Shenzhen Municipality, and Zhejiang Province to issue three or five year bonds.[89] The pilot program will be supervised by the Ministry of Finance, which will handle the servicing of the local government bonds. Each of the four local governments reportedly were provided a bond quota.[90] If successful, the pilot program may be expanded to include more local governments.

With respect to the risks associated with underground banking, after the Wenzhou crisis arose, China's financial regulators moved to stem the crisis and to monitor and regulate underground banking. In November 2011, the City of Wenzhou reportedly asked for $60 billion yuan ($9.4 billion) in financial stability support from the Zhejiang Provincial Government to help out local banks and companies damaged by the underground banking crisis.[91] In addition, the CBRC says it

---

[86] "China Tests to Check Rise of Cash Crunch Among Developers," *Bloomberg*, August 5, 2010.

[87] Wang Xiaotian, "Property Loan Risks Controllable: CBRC Chief," *China Daily*, October 20, 2011.

[88] China Banking Regulatory Commission, *Annual Report 2009*.

[89] Xing Yun, "Four Local Governments to Issue Bonds," *Caixin*, October 21, 2011.

[90] Ibid.

[91] Ma Guangyuan, "What Do We Have for Wenzhou's Rescue," *China-US Focus*, November 16, 2011.

has erected "firewalls" between China's financial institutions and underground lending to reduce the commercial banks' exposure to the underground banking risks.[92]

China's financial leaders are also considering their options for more long-term solutions to the underground banking problem. PBOC Governor Zhou sees a role for what he calls "informal financing" if it plays "a positive role in supporting the real economy," but opposes usury.[93] Other commentators say China needs to develop long-term finance vehicles to supplement the existing short-term, high interest funding currently available from Chinese banks.[94] Other alternatives being discussed are requiring the registration of all private loans and training banks to better assess the risks associated with lending to private companies.

Current Financial Situation of China's Banks

Despite the growing concern by the CBRC and market analysts, many observers considered the financial situation of China's banking sector at the end of 2010 to be reasonably strong (see **Table 13**). All the major types of banks were showing a profit and the NPL rate was quite low, particularly for a developing economy. Net profits were up 34.5% from the previous year; the value of NPLs was down 12.8%.[95] According to Asian Development Bank, China's ratio of NPLs to total loans as of June 2011 was 1.0%—higher than Hong Kong (0.6%) and Taiwan (0.5%), but lower than South Korea (1.6%) and Thailand (3.2%).[96]

Table 13. Financial Situation of Selected Types of Commercial Banks in China, 2010

Profitability and Non-Performing Loans (NPLs)

Type of Bank	After-Tax Profit	Return on Assets	Value of NPLs	NPLs as Share of Total Loans
Equitized Banks	515.1 billion yuan	1.1%	3125.5 billion yuan	1.3%
Joint-Stock Commercial Banks	135.8 billion yuan	0.9%	56.6 billion yuan	0.7%
City Commercial Banks	77.0 billion yuan	1.0%	32.6 billion yuan	0.9%
Rural Commercial Banks	28.0 billion yuan	1.0%	27.1 billion yuan	1.9%
Foreign Banks	7.8 billion yuan	0.4%	4.9 billion yuan	0.5%

Source: China Banking Regulatory Commission, *Annual Report 2011*.

Notes: Private banks are also referred to as joint-stock commercial banks

However, signs of underlying problems with China's banks continue to appear. Financial reports for a number of Chinese commercial banks for the first half of 2011 reported a notable increase in overdue loans.[97] Of the four equitized banks, only the Agricultural Bank of China did not report a

---

[92] "Local Go. Debts, Property Loans, Shadow Banking 'Controllable:' Banking Regulator," *Caijing*, October 20, 2011.

[93] Wang Xiaotian, "Informal Funding 'Can Support' Real Economy," *China Daily*, December 16-18, 2011.

[94] "Credit Crunch," *China Daily (USA Weekly)*, January 6-12, 2012.

[95] Wang Xiaotian, "Chinese Banks' Net Profit Up 34.5%: CBRC," *China Daily*, March 30, 2011.

[96] Asian Development Bank, *Asia Economic Monitor*, December 2011, p. 21.

[97] Wang Shenlu, "Commercial Banks See Rise in Overdue Loans," *Caixin*, August 30, 2011.

rise in overdue loans. A number of banks saw the value of their overdue loans rise by over 10% compared to a year ago. While overdue loans are technically not considered NPLs, the sharp increase was a cause of concern for CBRC and market analysts.

In June 2011, a report from China's National Audit Office (NAO) revealed that local government debt as of the end of 2010 exceeded 10.7 trillion yuan ($1.7 trillion).[98] A few days after the NAO results were disclosed, Moody's announced the results of their own estimates of local government debt in China, stating that the correct figure may be as high as 14.2 trillion yuan ($2.2 trillion).[99] As much as 1.84 trillion yuan ($290 billion) of the outstanding local debt will become due in 2012.[100] According to Moody's, China needs to develop a "clear master plan" to resolve the local debt problem, or China's banks will face a sharp rise in their NPL rates.[101]

Various market analysts have attempted to assess the local debt situation in China and its implications for China's banks. Fitch Ratings claims that the NPL rate in China is likely to rise to 5% and could reach 15%, depending on how well the Chinese government responds to the situation.[102] In a survey of financial institutions involved in the Chinese market, 84% of the respondents said that local government debt would create a major NPL problem sometime in the next two years, with the majority expecting the problem to emerge in 2013.[103] The average projection for the NPL rate among the respondents was 15%. A Credit Suisse study projected that the NPL rate in China will rise to 12% in the next few years and equal 60% of the value of total bank equity.[104]

The China's financial regulators appear to be preparing additional measures to reduce a sharp increase in NPLs and the resulting threat to the financial situation of China's banks. In April 2011, the CBRC said that banks needed to take steps to "prevent the loan risk associated with local government funding platforms."[105] In addition, the CBRC called for financial institutions to strictly abide by policies issued by the central government concerning lending practices for real estate and commercial loans. The Ministry of Finance was reportedly considering transferring 2-3 trillion yuan ($314 billion - $472 billion) of debt from the books of local governments partially to the central government and partially to "newly-created companies," but so far no action has been taken.[106] The CBRC is reportedly considering new regulations that would tie a bank's reserve requirement to the quality of its loan portfolio.[107] Other CBRC initiatives include reforming China's laws and regulations governing the closure of insolvent financial institutions, establishing a deposit insurance system, and further deregulation of interest rates. The CBRC is reportedly

---

[98] "China's Local Government Debts Exceed 10t Uuan," *China Daily*, June 27, 2011.

[99] "Moody's Sees Much Bigger Local Debt in China," *Reuters*, July 5, 2011.

[100] "China under Test with CBY1.84T Local Debts Dues in 2012," *Caijing*, February 13, 2012.

[101] "Moody's Sees Much Bigger Local Debt in China," *Reuters*, July 5, 2011

[102] "China Bank's Non-Performing Loans May Hit 15Pct; Fitch Ratings," *Caijing*, June 22, 2011.

[103] Lan Lan, "Local Debt NPL Problems Loom by 2013, Asset Manager's Poll Says," *China Daily*, September 20, 2011.

[104] Belinda Cao and Michael Patterson, "China Bad Debt May Reach 60% of Bank Equity, Credit Suisse Says," *Bloomberg*, October 12, 2011.

[105] China Banking Regulatory Commission, "The CBRC Held the Second Economic and Financial Situation Briefing of 2011," press release, May 9, 2011.

[106] "China to Clean Up Billions Worth of Local Debt," *Reuters*, May 31, 2011.

[107] Feng Zhe, "Bank Regulators Try Tailoring Bad-Debt Risk," *Caixin*, April 22, 2011.

---

also considering long-term extensions of bank loans to local governments.[108] The underlying principles for most of these changes appear to be making the banks responsible for their financial situation and lowering the central government's exposure to the potential cost of rescuing China's banks and local governments.

Allegations of Subsidized Loans

The media and reports about China's banking system are replete with allegations that Chinese banks provide subsidized loans to preferred companies – usually state-owned enterprises (SOEs) – as part of a central government strategy to make Chinese companies more domestically or globally competitive. Such claims are regularly made by the U.S. government, U.S. businesses, scholars, and others. The Chinese government acknowledges that past financial policies did provide SOEs with preferential loans, but asserts that the recent banking reforms have effectively ended these policies and that lending is now being done on a commercial basis. Some scholars maintain that recent lending patterns – particularly after the 2007 global financial crisis – provide evidence that the central government by and large no longer directs banks to provide preferential credit to SOEs, and that banks are extending credit largely on a commercial basis.

The alleged bank subsidies of SOEs in China has become one of the issues raised in the larger discussion of China's supposed unfair competitive practices in world trade. The World Trade Organization's Agreement on Subsidies and Countervailing Measures defines a subsidy as financial contribution by a government or public body within the territory of a WTO member, which confers a benefit.[109] To be WTO actionable, the subsidy must be shown to have an adverse effect on the complaining WTO member, either by injuring its domestic industry, diminishing the value of some form of trade benefit (e.g. – preferential tariffs), or seriously prejudicing its interests.

U.S. Government Allegations of Chinese Bank Subsidies

The U.S. government has released evidence of it argues demonstrates the Chinese government is providing subsidies by means of credit. It has submitted a request to the World Trade Organization's (WTO) Committee on Subsidies and Countervailing Measures for information on possible Chinese subsidies. In addition, the International Trade Administration (ITA) has on several occasions considered countervailing duty (CVD) petitions containing claims that China is providing actionable credit or loan subsidies.

WTO Request

On October 11, 2011, the U.S. government submitted to the WTO Committee on Subsidies and Countervailing Measures a request that the Committee be notified of approximately 200 possibly non-compliant subsidies provided by China's central and local governments to Chinese enterprises.[110] Of the cases listed in the request, seven explicitly refer to either preferential

---

[108] Chen Jia and Wang Xiaotian, "CBRC Weighs Debt Extensions," *China Daily*, February 14, 2012.

[109] For more details about WTO agreements and subsidies, see CRS Report R40606, *Trade Remedies and the WTO Rules Negotiations*, by Vivian C. Jones

[110] U.S. government, *Request for the United States to China Pursuant to Article 25.10 of the Agreement*, WTO (continued...)

---

policies of the CBRC or interest or loan subsidies.[111] The documents in question require Chinese banks to establish special procedures to review credit applications made under central government programs designed to promote "major national scientific and technological projects" or "hi-tech enterprises." However, the documents also contain language explicitly stating that any credit provided should be based on various commercial criteria. The documents do not contain any direct statement that the enterprises in question should be given preferential credit terms.

CVD Petitions

Allegations that the Chinese government is providing preferential loan programs to selected Chinese enterprises are also found in CVD petitions submitted to the ITA. The ITA has been conducting CVD claims against China since 2007. Many of the CVD petitions include allegations that Chinese enterprises are receiving various forms of loan or credit subsidies. Among the types of subsidies most frequently mentioned are: preferential loans to SOEs; preferential loans for "key projects;" preferential lending to "honorable enterprises;" discount loans for export-oriented enterprises; and special provincial loan programs. However, the preliminary ITA assessments generally have stated that the petitioners provided insufficient evidence to warrant investigation into the loan subsidy claims.

One notable CVD case was a 2007 petition regarding coated free sheet paper from China. In a memorandum regarding the market economy status of the industry, the ITA determined that China's history of non-performing loans to SOEs – and the tendency to allocate a disproportionate share of credit to SOEs – had previously constituted evidence of the continuing non-market economy status of China.[112] However, the memorandum continued by pointing to various aspects of China's economic reforms, including reforms of its banking system, as being sufficient to consider CVD petitions against China.

Other Allegations

A number of scholars and other analysts of China's financial markets argue that the State utilizes Chinese banks to provide state-owned enterprises and other selected companies with preferential loans. In its 2011 Report to Congress, the U.S.-China Economic and Security Review Commission wrote, "China's largest banks are state-owned and are required by the central government to make loans to state-owned companies at below market interest rates and, in some cases, to forgive those loans."[113] On February 15, 2012, Elizabeth J. Drake, a Partner with the Law Offices of Stewart and Stewart, stated in her testimony at a hearing of the U.S.-China Economic and Security Review Commission, "SOEs in China enjoy significant advantages due to their preferential access to credit and debt forgiveness from state-owned banks …"[114] According

---

(...continued)

document G/SCM/Q2/CHN/42, October 11, 2011.

[111] Most of the alleged subsidies take the form of preferential tax treatments.

[112] Office of Policy, Import Administration, International Trade Administration, *Countervailing Duty Investigation of Coated Free Sheet*, C-570-907, March 29, 2007.

[113] U.S.-China Economic and Security Review Commission, *2011 Report to Congress*, Washington, DC, November 2011, p. 46.

[114] Elizabeth J. Drake, "Chinese State-owned and State-controlled Enterprises: Policy Options for Addressing Chinese State-owned Enterprises," testimony before the U.S.-China Economic and Security Commission, February 15, 2012.

to Drake, concessional export credits and export credit guarantees provided by China Development Bank and China Ex-Im Bank are major sources of State-directed financial subsidies for SOEs, totaling as much as $100 billion per year – about the total cumulative exposure limit for the U.S. Export-Import Bank.

Song Ligang, Associate Professor of Economics at the Australian National University, presents a more mixed picture of China's banking subsidies for SOEs.[115] According to Song, "Interest rate controls have served to maintain the market dominance of state banks, which have long directed most of their lending to state-owned enterprises." In short, the combination of a state policy (interest rate controls) and lending bias by the state banks have resulted in a de facto subsidization of SOEs. In addition, Song maintains that the failure of non-state financial institutions to emerge has led to the continuation of the unintended subsidies.

Adam S. Hersh, an economist at the Center for American Progress, offered a third understanding of bank subsidy issue in his testimony before the U.S.-China Economic and Security Review Commission.[116] According to Hersh, local government officials – not the central government – are the predominant source of outside influence in the allocation of credit by Chinese banks. Hersh stated in his testimony, "(L)ocal government officials have directed this support to both government-owned and private-owned companies with a goal of promoting overall economic and export growth." In his assessment, Hersh maintained, "not all domestic bank credit is used to support SOEs on a non-commercial basis. World Bank economists Robert Cull and Collin Xu find that firms receiving bank loans in China tend to be of higher productivity."

A recent book, *Inside China, Inc.*, focuses on the role of China Development Bank (CDB) in the overseas investments by Chinese enterprises in energy and natural resources.[117] The author, Erica Downs, a research fellow at the Brookings Institute, generally downplays the notion that lower interest rates imply loan subsidies, stating:

> The fact that CDB may be lending at interest rates lower than what a western bank might require does not mean that it acts simply as an agent of state policy with no regard to profit. Instead, CDB balances its commitment to profitability and its mandate to advance the policy priorities of the Chinese government. On a straight commercial basis, it may be rational for CDB to accept lower interest rates than western banks because CDB is backed by the Chinese government.[118]

China's Response

Chinese officials and bank officers acknowledge that in the past the central government played an active role in the allocation of loans and credit, and that SOEs were provided preferential terms over other types of enterprises, generally in the form of lower interest rates or debt forgiveness.

---

[115] Song Ligang, "Interest Rate Liberalization in China and the Implications for Non-state Banks," Chapter 7, *Financial Sector Reform in China*, edited by Huang Yasheng, Tony Saich, and Edward Steinfeld, Harvard University Asia Center, Cambridge, MA, 2005.

[116] Adam S. Hersh, "Testimony before the U.S.-China Economic and Security Review Commission on 'Chinese State-owned and State-controlled Enterprises," testimony before the U.S.-China Economic and Security Commission, February 15, 2012.

[117] Erica Downs, *Inside China, Inc.: China Development Bank's Cross-Border Energy Deals* (Washington , DC: Brookings Institution, 2011).

[118] Ibid., p. 62.

However, in interviews with CRS, they contend that since the "equitization" of most of the previously state-owned banks and the reform of bank management policy, the newly-established Chinese commercial banks autonomously decide to whom to provide commercial loans.[119]

Xiao Gang, chairman of the Bank of China, echoes the response of Chinese banking officials in an article he wrote in 2010.[120] Following a rapid rise on bank lending, Xiao notes, "Many people have reason to believe that China's lending spree last year ...was the result of government intervention. The evidence seems obvious – the government holds controlling stakes in those banks and appoints the chairpersons and the CEOs." However, Xiao asserts, "Since the major State-owned banks have undergone a process of commercialization, from financial restructuring to forming foreign strategic partnerships to going public, they have generated a strong internal and market-driven desire to increase their lending. *They did not act on government orders* [emphasis added]." Later on, Xiao is more emphatic in his denial of government intervention in bank lending practices, stating, "As a chairman of a bank, I have never received any instructions from the government to lend money to any project. All decisions relating to business were made either by the board, or by the management."

The Historical Evidence

The claims that the Chinese government is directing Chinese banks to provide preferential loans to selected enterprises generally relies on two types of financial evidence: 1. that the selected enterprises are being provided a disproportional share of loans or credit; and 2. that the terms of the loans being provided to the selected enterprises are based on preferential treatment, usually in the form of lower interest rates. In addition, to demonstrate that the greater access and preferential terms of the loans constitute a government subsidy, it has to be shown that the loans are not based on commercial considerations, but are the result of the Chinese government directing the banks to provide the preferential loans. What follows is a separate examination of the available data for credit access and interest rates for China's SOEs, and within those sections, a discussion of the issue of government direction of bank lending behavior.

Access to Credit

One of the key forms of evidence of Chinese banks subsidizing SOEs is the reported disproportionate share of credit extended to SOEs relative to other forms of enterprises in China. Almost 70% of state-owned commercial bank new loan commitments in 2001 were given to SOEs, according to Pieter Bottelier.[121] According to the PBOC, "loans to non-financial enterprises and other sectors" – a proxy some scholars use to estimate loans to SOEs and local government funding platforms – totaled 5.04 trillion yuan ($793 billion), or 67.5% of total new loans for the year, which is slightly lower than Bottlier's estimate for 2001.

In addition, some observers claim that the SOE's preferential access to credit increased when the Chinese government implemented a stimulus package following the 2007 global financial

---

[119] CRS interviews conducted with Chinese banking regulators and senior bank officials conducted in 2010 and 2011.

[120] Xiao Gang, "Don't Blame It on the Government," press release, Bank of China, August 26, 2010.

[121] Pieter Bottelier, " Managing China's Transition Debt: Challenges for Sustained Development," Chapter 6, *Financial Sector Reform in China*, edited by Huang Yasheng, Tony Saich, and Edward Steinfeld, Harvard University Asia Center, Cambridge, MA, 2005.

crisis.[122] However, Nicholas R. Lardy, a research fellow at the Peterson Institute for International Economics, maintains, "(C)ontrary to the often repeated assertion, bank loans in 2009-10 did not flow primarily to state-owned companies and that the access of both private firms and household businesses to bank credit improved considerably."[123] In addition to be provided more than their fair share of credit, the SOEs supposedly have been subsidized by greater forgiveness of outstanding debt.

The Chinese government has taken steps that appear to be in response to criticisms that SOEs are being provided a disproportionate share of commercial credit. The CBRC issued a new regulation in October 2011 designed to provide greater incentives to Chinese banks to offer loans to small enterprises.[124] The new regulation allows banks to deduct loans of under 5 million yuan ($786,000) to small enterprises from the calculation of the bank's loan-deposit ratio, as well as reduces the weight of loans to small enterprises in calculating the bank's asset risk. The goal of the new regulation is to raise the growth rate for loans to small enterprises above the national growth rate of commercial loans.

Other factors may also be influencing how Chinese banks allocate credit among potential borrowers. The three remaining policy banks – ADBC, CDB, and China ExIm Bank – remain under the direct control of the central government and are mandated to provide credit to support national development projects, and thus are more likely to provide loans to large SOEs chosen to head these projects. The "equitized" commercial banks have a history of lending to SOEs when they were fully state-owned, and may be more comfortable with lending to known clients than to new, and possibly riskier private enterprises. Similarly, city commercial banks have historically served as a major source of credit for local governments and local enterprises, leading the bank management to focus on their known clientele at the expense of smaller, newer private companies.

Interest Rates

The other major form of evidence frequently cited to support claims of Chinese banks subsidizing SOEs is the claim that SOEs are generally provided loans at lower interest rates than other types of companies in China. Because China does not report information on effective interest rates on commercial loans by type of enterprise, attempts to substantiate this claim have relied on independently compiled data based on information on individual loans available in the Chinese or international press. Such studies are inherently incomplete in their coverage, but may indicate if the claims have any basis in the observable data.

It is generally agreed that prior to the initiation of financial reforms in 1997, the Chinese government fixed interest rates for both bank deposits and loans. [125] In addition, Chinese banks

---

[122] For example, Jason Leow, "China Loans Hard to Get – Smaller Enterprises Left Dry as Bulk of Lending Goes to Big Projects," *Wall Street Journal*, May, 14, 2009.

[123] Nicholas R. Lardy, *Sustaining China's Economic Growth After the Global Financial Crisis* (Washington, DC: Peterson Institute for International Economics, 2012), p. 1. For more details of Lardy's evidence, see Chapter 1: China's Reponse to the Global Crisis, pp. 5-42.

[124] The full text of "The Supplementary Circular on Supporting Commercial Banks to Further Improve Their Financial Services to Micro and Small-sized Enterprises" is available online (in Chinese) at: http://www.cbrc.gov.cn/chinese/ home/docDOC_ReadView/20111025F37A5341A99DC5A4FF3C903C0A953000 html

[125] For more information on the history of interest rate reform in China, see Nicholas R. Lardy, *Sustaining China's Economic Growth After the Global Financial Crisis* (Washington, DC: Peterson Institute for International Economics, (continued...)

---

were required to provide loans to SOEs at fixed interest rates lower than those extended to other types of enterprises. In the following years, interest rates on loans were gradually liberalized, allowing banks to determine the interest rate for a particular loan within a given range of a benchmark interest rate set by the PBOC (see **Table 4**). Eventually, the PBOC eliminated the ceiling on interest rates, but continued to set a benchmark interest rate. Throughout this period, the PBOC continued to set fixed interest rates for bank deposits.

Caixin, an independent online economic news agency in China, reported in March 2011 that Unirule, an independent think tank in Beijing, had conducted a study of SOEs and determined that "the average annual interest rate for SOEs was 1.6 percent while the annual rate for private companies was 5.4 percent."[126] However, an examination of the original Unirule report (in Chinese) reveals that the study, covering the years 2001 to 2005, estimated the effective interest rate paid on loans by dividing declared interest payments by the value of outstanding loans for each enterprise. The report's table show that the SOEs effective interest rate varied from 2.46% to 2.86%, while effective interest rate for private enterprises varied from 3.81% to 4.84%. For the five years covered in the Unirule report, the difference between the SOE and private enterprise effective interest rate varies from 0.95% to 2.41%.

A 2009 study by the Hong Kong Institute for Monetary Policy used a different approach to determine if SOEs received preferential loan treatment by Chinese banks.[127] Using National Bureau of Statistics information for about 160,000 Chinese firms, the study compared the cost of debt (interest payments/outstanding loans) for SOEs to other types of ownership. The study found that SOEs were charged 225 basis points (0.225%) less than private companies and 157 basis points (0.157%) less than the average interest rate in the selected sample. According to the authors, "The low costs of debt for SOEs seem to be neither justified on the grounds of better productivity nor on the basis of lower leverage…" However, the authors also note, "Obviously, the low costs of debt for SOEs might be explained by other factors.[128] For instance, a major expected difference between the SOEs and private enterprises is asset size…the data confirms that the costs of debt are noticeably lower as the firm size increases." The authors conclude, "(O)ur estimates show that if SOEs were to pay a market interest rate [i.e. – the same interest rate as private enterprises], their existing profits would be entirely wiped out. Our findings suggest that SOEs are still benefiting from credit subsidies and they are not yet subject to the market interest rates."

The authors also note two other important issues related to the issue of the alleged subsidization of SOEs by Chinese banks. They state in the introduction to the study, "It is well known that SOEs in China are quite reluctant to pay back their loans to SOCBs [State-Owned Chinese banks]." It is possible that the failure of SOEs to service their loans – thereby generating NPLs – may constitute a larger source of subsidization to SOEs in China than the alleged interest rate

---

(…continued)

2012), p. 83-85.

[126] Wang Jing, "Unirule: SOEs Register Negative Real Profits," *Caixin*, March 3, 2011.

[127] Giovanni Ferri and Li-Gang Liu, "Honor Thy Creditors Beforan Thy Shareholders: Are the Profits of Chinese State-Owned Enterprises Real?," *Hong Kong Institute for Monetary Policy*, HKIMR Working Paper No. 16/2009, 2009.

[128] The authors acknowledge that their study and its findings are based on some debatable assumptions and analysis. First, the use of the private enterprise interest rate as a proxy for the market interest rate is questionable. Second, the specification of the econometric model, and particularly the variables included in the estimations, may result in misattribution of the sources of interest rate differentials. Third, while the authors note that the SOE's lower interest rates may be provided because of other commercial factors – some identified by the authors – not included in the study.

preferences. In addition, the authors observe that the relations between SOCBs and SOEs has historically been "politically influenced," implying that considerations other than commercial merit have affected the allocation of credit in China.

Lardy offers an alternative explanation for the seemingly low interest rate loans Chinese banks provide to SOEs and other companies.[129] Although the PBOC has eliminated the ceiling on bank lending rates, it has continued to fix the interest rate on deposits, with a built-in 2-3% margin (see **Table 4**). According to Lardy, "The government's policy of low interest rates on deposits indirectly depresses interest rates on loans. This occurs largely because of competition among banks."

China's leadership apparently intend to continue to liberalize interest rates, but it is uncertain when and in what fashion this will occur. PBOC Governor Zhou wrote a speech on December 17, 2010 in which he laid out the reasons why China wanted to promote "market-based interest rate reform."[130] In his speech, Zhou argued:

> (T)he key to market-based interest rate reform is that financial institutions have autonomy to price their products. Since the onset of reform, autonomy of enterprises has always been emphasized, including the essential pricing autonomy. As a result of the reforms, all financial institutions but policy ones operate on a fully commercial basis, and an important part of their autonomy is to independently price their products and services.

Late in 2011, the PBOC's Monetary Policy Committee met in Beijing and decided to make efforts to "promote the market-based reform of the interest rates."[131] No details were provided on what measures would be taken. On January 19, 2012, China Daily ran a story in which Li Mingxian, President of Guangdong Development Bank, called for the removal of the interest rate ceiling on time deposits of longer than one year duration.[132]

Implications for Congress

At present, two main aspects of China's banking systems may have significant implications for Sino-U.S. relations and by extension, for Congress. First, China's policies on credit and loans have been cited as a source of subsidization for Chinese companies, making it difficult for U.S. companies to compete in global markets. Congress could consider various options with respect to evaluating and responding to allegations of inappropriate bank subsidies in China. Second, China's intention to further liberalize its financial sector—including the further deregulation of interest rates – may create greater opportunities for U.S. banks and financial institutions to enter China's domestic market. However, domestic concerns about inflation may make Chinese officials cautious about implementing reforms that could lead to higher interest rates. Congress could look into ways of encouraging banking reforms in China that would be conducive to greater market penetration for U.S. banks.

---

[129] Nicholas R. Lardy, *Sustaining China's Economic Growth After the Global Financial Crisis* (Washington, DC: Peterson Institute for International Economics, 2012), pp. 78-86.

[130] Zhou Xiaochuan, "A Few Thoughts on Market-based Interest Rate Reform," a speech written on December 17, 2010, presented in January 2011. Available online at PBOC's webpage: http://www.pbc.gov.cn/.

[131] People's Bank of China, "PBC's Monetary Policy Committee Held its 4th Quarterly Meeting in 2011," press release, January 5, 2012.

[132] Han Tianyang, "Banker: Flexibility Needed in Deposit and Loan Rates," *China Daily*, January 19, 2012.

Responding to Inappropriate Bank Subsidies

Under current U.S. law, the primary means by which U.S. entities can seek relief from perceived inappropriate bank subsidies in China is by submitting a CVD petition. In order for the bank subsidy to be considered in the CVD determination, the subsidy must either be a prohibited or actionable subsidy.[133] For several years, some Members of Congress have advocated the reexamination of U.S. trade remedy laws. The 112th Congress may consider modifying U.S. laws governing CVD petitions to include specific provisions regarding preferential loans, unwarranted credit provision, non-payment of loans, and other means by which banks can subsidize companies.

In addition, Congress may chose to press the Obama Administration to respond to allegations of inappropriate bank lending practices at such fora as the Strategic and Economic Dialogues (S&ED) and the Joint Committee on Commerce and Trade (JCCT) meetings. Furthermore, Congress may consider asking the U.S. Department of the Treasury to investigate the lending practices of Chinese banks to determine to what extent the banking sector is operating on a commercial basis and if Chinese banks are a significant source of subsidization of Chinese enterprises and investment. Congress may also seek greater U.S. efforts to address bank subsidization at multilateral fora, such as the G20, as well as part of the on-going Doha Round negotiations.

Financial Liberalization and WTO Compliance

In his report to the National People's Congress March 2009, Premier Wen Jiabao called for the continuation of banking reforms in China. The reform of state-owned financial institutions were to be "deepened," and small and medium-sized financial institutions were to be "steadily" developed under "multiple forms of ownership." On December 31, 2010, however, PBOC Governor Zhou stated that while efforts would be made to continue financial reforms in 2011, the prevention of systemic risks and safeguarding financial stability would be priorities in China's monetary policy.[134] It is unclear how China will balance Wen's call for further reforms with Zhou's concerns about financial stability.

If implemented, Wen's proposed reforms may provide an opportunity for U.S. banks and other financial service providers to enter China's financial market. The exchange of information and ideas on possible reforms in China's banking sector may be a productive topic for future bilateral talks. The topics of China's banking reforms and China's compliance with its WTO accession agreement have been raised at past Strategic and Economic Dialogues (S&ED), as well as Joint Committee on Commerce and Trade (JCCT) meetings, and are likely to continue to be raised by the United States at future bilateral fora. It is also likely that China, for its part, will continue to raise its concerns about market access for Chinese banks in the United States. Chinese officials have claimed in the past that U.S. procedures for approving foreign bank branches is needlessly complex and that selective enforcement has discriminated against Chinese banks.

---

[133] For more information on the criteria for consideration of CVD petitions, see CRS Report RL32371, *Trade Remedies: A Primer*, by Vivian C. Jones.

[134] "China's Central Bank Reiterates Monetary Policy Stance in 2011," *Xinhua*, December 31, 2010.

The 111th Congress passed the Dodd-Frank Wall Street Reform and Consumer Protection Act (P.L. 111-203), which, among other things, created a Bureau of Consumer Financial Protection within the Federal Reserve and consolidated bank regulation by merging the Office of Thrift Supervision (OTS) into the Office of the Comptroller of the Currency (OCC). China monitored congressional consideration of this act closely. Based on meetings with Chinese officials, one of their main concerns was how the new law would affect U.S. compliance with Basel III.[135] It is possible that any additional reforms in China's financial system may reflect lessons learnt from Chinese officials' analysis of the Dodd-Frank Wall Street Reform and Consumer Protection Act.

The extent to which the 112th Congress may choose to play a role in this issue remains to be seen. Under current law, Congress is to be advised on the proceedings of major bilateral meetings, such as the S&ED and the JCCT. In addition, the USTR is required to provide Congress with an annual report on China's WTO compliance. Congress could, if it should so choose, hold hearings or request briefings on China's financial reforms and their implications for U.S. market access. In addition, Congress could consider legislation designed to encourage or require China to fulfill its WTO obligations with respect to opening its financial services sector to foreign banks.

---

[135] Basel III is an agreement on capital requirements among countries' central banks and bank supervisory authorities. The agreement is not treaty; member countries – which includes the United States – man modify the agreement to suite their financial regulatory structures. For more about Basel III and the U.S. financial system, see CRS Report R41467, *The Status of the Basel III Capital Adequacy Accord*, by Walter W. Eubanks.

Appendix. List of Chinese Banks by Type

Type of Bank	Names of Banks
State-owned (3)	Agricultural Development Bank of China, China Development Bank, Export-Import Bank of China
Equitized (5)	Agricultural Bank of China, Bank of China, Bank of Communications, China Construction Bank, Industrial and Commercial Bank of China
Joint-stock (12)	China Bohai Bank, China Citic Bank, China Everbright Bank, China Merchants Bank, China Minsheng Bank, China Zheshang Bank, Evergrowing Bank, Guangdong Development Bank, Hua Xia Bank, Industrial Bank, Shanghai Pudong Development Bank, Shenzhen Development Bank
Local (92)	Anshan City Commercial Bank, Baotou City Commercial Bank, Bank of Beijing, Cangzhou City Commercial Bank, Changchun City Commercial Bank, Changsha City Commercial Bank, Chengdu City Commercial Bank, Chengde City Commercial Bank, Bank of Chongqing, Bank of Dalian, Dan Dong City Commercial Bank, Daqing City Commercial Bank, Deyang City Commercial Bank, Dezhou City Commercial Bank, Dongying City Commercial Bank, Fuzhou City Commercial Bank, Fushun Commercial Bank, Fuxin City Commercial Bank, Ganzhou City Commercial Bank, Guiyang Commercial Bank, Guilin City Commercial Bank, Harbin City Commercial Bank, Hangzhou City Commercial Bank, Hengyang City Commercial Bank, Huhhot City Commercial Bank, Huludao City Commercial Bank, Huzhou City Commercial Bank, Huangshi City Commercial Bank, Huishang Bank Corporation, Jilin City Commercial Bank, Jinan City Commercial Bank, Jiaxing City Commercial Bank, Bank of Jiangsu, Commercial Bank of Jiaozuo, Jinhua City Commercial Bank, Jin Zhou City Commercial Bank, Jingzhou City Commercial Bank, Jiujiang City Commercial Bank, Kunming City Commercial Bank, Laiwu City Commercial Bank, Lanzhou City Commercial Bank, Langfang City Commercial Bank, Leshan City Commercial Bank, Liaoyang City Commercial Bank, Liuzhou City Commercial Bank, Luzhou City Commercial Bank, Commercial Bank of Luoyang, Mudanjiang City Commercial Bank, Nanchang City Commercial Bank, Bank of Nanjing, Nanning City Commerce Bank, Bank of Ningbo, Ordos Commercial Bank, Panjin City Commercial Bank, Qiqihar City Commercial Bank, Qinhuangdao City Commercial Bank, Qingdao City Commercial Bank, Qujing City Commercial Bank, Quanzhou City Commercial Bank, Rizhao City Commercial Bank, Bank of Shanghai, Shangrao City Commercial Bank, Shaoxing City Commercial Bank, Shenzhen Pingan Bank, Shengjing Bank, Shijiazhuang City Commercial Bank, Taizhou City Commercial Bank, Tang Shan City Commercial Bank, Bank of Tianjin, Tieling Commerial Bank, Weifang City Commercial Bank, Wenzhou City Commercial Bank, Wuhai City Commercial Bank, Urumqi City Commercial Bank, Wuhan Urban Commercial Bank, Xiamen City Commercial Bank, Xiang Tan City Commercial Bank, Xiangfan City Commercial Bank, Xiaogan City Commercial Bank, Xinxiang City Commercial Bank, Yantai City Commercial Bank, Yichang City Commercial Bank, Yinchuan City Commercial Bank, Yingkou Commercial Bank, Yuxi City Commercial Bank, Yueyang City Commercial Bank, Zhangjiakou City Commercial Bank, Zhejiang Chouzhou Commercial Bank, Zhejiang Mintai Commercial Bank, Zhejiang Tailong Commercial Bank, Zhuzhou City Commercial Bank, Zunyi City Commercial Bank

Source: China Banking Regulatory Commission web page

Notes: Table does not include the Postal Savings Bank of China, which is owned by the China Postal Group, the business entity created following the restructuring of China's State Postal Bureau in 2007.

Author Contact Information

Michael F. Martin
Specialist in Asian Affairs
mfmartin@crs.loc.gov, 7-2199

www.ingramcontent.com/pod-product-compliance
Lightning Source LLC
Chambersburg PA
CBHW080614290526
45790CB00007B/2767